ADVANCE

DESTINATION NEW EARTH

"As a channel of metaphysical books, I loved *Destination New Earth*. I used to work with Autistic kids and could feel a deeper communication wanting to break through with them, so the content really resonated with me. If you are new to metaphysical books, I would suspend your disbelief as you read and keep an open mind—you won't be disappointed. Many things are not as they seem, and this book takes you on a deeper dive with some beautiful content and mind-expanding concepts. The more seasoned mystical reader will not be disappointed either. This take on channeling and telepathy is pertinent as we go deeper into ascension and the collective, becoming more aware of our divine selves. What a time to be alive. Thank you for this book and your contribution to awakening and the raising of human consciousness."

—Robbie Mackenzie, Channel for Metatron,
Author of *Metatron, This Is the Clarion Call*

"Have you ever wondered what all this New Earth stuff is about anyway?! This thought-provoking book will answer some of those questions you've had, even some you didn't realise you had! As a parent to an autistic child with ADHD, I resonate with the vision of these special members of humanity as being the next step in our evolutionary process and harbingers of the New Earth. *Destination New Earth* clarified that vision and helped me see even more of the bigger picture. A great read!"

—Rachel Goodwin, Channel for Ascended Master Sarah, Author of *Sarah's Little Book of Healing*

"*Destination New Earth is a gift!* It is witness to the realization of spiritual awareness of autist consciousness and the wisdom of the ages. It is a blueprint and guide for the times we are living in. It asks us to wake up and raise our frequency to the wisdom of harmonic love. Allow yourself to soak in every word, for the sacredness of the exposure and inquiry from each word reveals a greater advancement of cosmic truth of individuals and our New Earth."

—Rev. Dr. Patty Luckenbach, Author of *The Land of Tears* and *I Only Walk on Water When It Rains*

DESTINATION
New Earth

A Blueprint to 5D Consciousness

ALEX MARCOUX

with Shauna Kalicki, Daniel, and Connie

Destination New Earth: A Blueprint to 5D Consciousness
By Alex Marcoux, with Shauna Kalicki, Daniel, and Connie

Paperback: 978-1-7352611-7-1
Library of Congress Number: 2021923458

First paperback edition

Edited by Donna Mazzitelli, Writing With Donna
Proofreading by Delta Donohue, Proofing Pages LLC
Cover art and layout by Victoria Wolf, wolfdesignandmarketing.com
Cover image by Laurie Bain of Primal Painter, www.primalpainter.com

Printed in the USA.
616 Editions, an Imprint of Jenness

P.O. Box 620681
Littleton, CO 80162

This book is dedicated to all those on the path.

OTHER BOOKS BY ALEX MARCOUX

NOVELS

The Unsuspected Heroes: A Visionary Fiction Novel
A Matter of Degrees
Back to Salem
Facades

NONFICTION

Lifesigns: Tapping the Power of Synchronicity,
Serendipity and Miracles

CONTRIBUTING AUTHOR

50 Great Writers You Should be Reading
Awakening and Applying Intuition and Psychic Ability

CONTENTS

FOREWORD

Letter from Connie

Dear Reader,

My name is Connie, and I'm delighted to be a part of this project to share information with humanity. Not too long ago, I was highly skeptical and only believed what my eyes saw—until my autistic son, Daniel, "came out of the closet" with his spiritual gifts. He and the Autist Collective have converted me. I have witnessed magic firsthand during these chaotic times. The Autists have been great educators and guides to the New Earth.

From the beginning, after I learned about my son, he was adamant that he needed to share his knowledge about the New Earth with the world and wanted me to be his voice. Being the shy gal that I am, I outright refused. *How could I do this? What platform would I use? Who would believe me?*

I got involved with this project because of the sincerity of the others involved: the author Alex Marcoux, the channel

Shauna Kalicki, and my son gently nudged me to put my energy into this book. It is time to share and for me to come out of my shell. I no longer fear being ridiculed or perceived as crazy, nor should any of you. What is crazy is to accept the information being fed to you simply because the majority agrees with it.

It is time for humanity to have a new and different experience to discover the New Earth. This book will permit readers to learn about it and realize that they are in it and need to relish its beauty.

I am the transcriber of the channeling sessions involved with this project. I provide structure to the sessions by creating follow-up questions for clarity. I have read many New Age, spiritual, and New Thought books and was often left scratching my head confused about what I just read. I wished someone could break it down for me in an easier-to-understand way.

Our group made every effort to make this book easy to understand, especially for those new to this "woo" spiritual world. Yet, we trust that those who have been on the path will find jewels within also.

Most importantly, this book was created and written with love and integrity. I utilized my intuition to discern the information coming through the channel and validated that information through Daniel, who uses a plastic communication board to communicate. The Autist Collective is a group of "silent" heroes who have been ushering in the New Earth and shedding light for humanity to witness this birthing and reveal how *genuinely divine you are*. As you read this book, I hope you experience the joy, magic, and love that went into its creation.

It is truly an honor to be here in these epic times with each one of you. This project has been a wonderful learning experience for me, and I hope it is for you.

As I finished typing this message to you, I asked Daniel if he wanted to share something with the readers.

He typed on my laptop keyboard, `"Welcome home."` He is welcoming you to the New Earth, and let this book be your guide.

Much love,
Connie

Letter from Shauna Kalicki

Dear Reader,

Welcome to this book and perhaps some interesting insights for you to ponder. I have known Connie, Daniel, and Alex since 2016. We have shared many magical moments. Some have been intense, while others have been whimsical— yet all have been life-changing for me.

Alex asked if I would channel for this book. Admittedly, at first, while I was comfortable tapping the information for our small group and myself, I hadn't shared it with others like you. Throughout my life, I have experienced insights and wisdom from Archangels, some Ethereal Autists, and Ascended

Masters, particularly the Magdalenes. In 2018, I began channeling Cerian, a sixteenth-dimensional collective. Sharing
this information with the world was a bit of a leap for me and,
ultimately, my gift to you.

This book is an endeavor of love and carries hope and
encouragement for each of us. Remember to surrender to your
True Self.

In light, love, and service,
Shauna

ACKNOWLEDGMENTS

I AM GRATEFUL TO THOSE drawn to this book. Yes, you, the reader, for you are in fifth-dimensional consciousness. You have shown up to do the work. This book is part of your spiritual awakening. Whether you consider yourself awake, partially awake, or not awake, Daniel shares, "This book is a bridge to understanding a new perspective. *Be open to the miracles it will ignite within.*" What you do with this knowledge is choice, though our group hopes you seek, live your spiritual blueprint, and share this material with people of like minds. That is how this book will get into the right hands, specifically, those on a path of ascension.

I thank our team for their contributions to this book—their friendship and coming into my life. Shauna, for your willing-ness, abilities, and commitment to channeling. Connie, for the endless hours of transcriptions, reading, guidance, and seeking clarification from Daniel. Daniel, for your patience with me, for showing up big, and for everything you do for humanity. I am grateful for those beings who provided messages, particularly Daniel, Mother Mary, and Cerian. I am thankful for the Autist Collective and all their work and all beings involved in this great awakening.

I can't thank my editor enough, Donna Mazzitelli, for taking a personal interest in our project and going beyond the call of duty. Thank you, Delta Donohue, for your proofing, Victoria Wolf, for the magnificent cover and layout. I am grateful to Laurie Bain of Primal Painter for her extraordinary vision and artwork in designing the cover image.

I thank Team Blue Ray for holding space and energetically supporting the birth of this project. Che, for reading and suggesting, namaste.

I am grateful to my son for his love. I cannot thank Robyn enough for her love and for permitting me space to write and be me. To my family and friends, those named and unnamed, who have supported me in this journey, you are my heroes, and I love you all.

INTRODUCTION

All great truths begin as blasphemies.
—George Bernard Shaw

THERE IS A SHIFT IN CONSCIOUSNESS occurring on our planet. We are witnessing and experiencing the spiritual evolution of humanity. Many await the prophesized return of Jesus, or the Second Coming, for the last Day of Judgment. Some also expect the emergence of the New Heavens and New Earth as being the final state of redeemed humanity.

What if no savior is coming? What if the New Earth is already here? What if you only need to shift your perspective to experience it? And what if "all this" is a game to see if you awaken to the truth about who you are?

Destination New Earth depicts conversations between the Masters and me. The "Masters" I refer to are Mother Mary, an Ethereal Autist named Daniel, and Cerian, a higher-dimensional consciousness speaking through one voice. Some of these dialogues occurred while Shauna Kalicki, a psychic medium, channeled the beings. Other discussions occurred while Connie asked her son, Daniel, to verify or expand on topics emerging in the channeling sessions.

The channeling sessions were prearranged to answer questions (unknown to the channel) about the New Earth. The emerged conversations took us in surprising directions, challenged my New Thought beliefs, and brought up information we believe humanity needs to hear.

Within this text, I dialogue with Ascended Masters about the New Earth and the role of Autists in humanity's spiritual evolution. The content explores the energetic connection between ancient peoples throughout time, revealing that the fall in consciousness in Lemuria and Atlantis was intentional and that this life is a game we chose to play. Or did we? What if, to remain in control, some didn't play by the rules at the game's onset?

The evolution of humanity begins with each awakening to their authentic self and living their divine blueprint. Each person has a unique role to play in this spiritual evolution. When we awaken to our purpose and live authentically, we become part of a much larger plan to assist humanity in this journey to the New Earth.

There is a spiritual war occurring. It is a real war and has real casualties: those surrendering their sovereignty. Without reaching a critical mass of people who awaken, humanity's evolution is at risk. Some parties fight to assist humanity in this spiritual evolution, while others attempt to control humankind and prevent people from awakening to their true selves.

Each person has a role in this journey. *If your part is to evolve in this consciousness shift, this book is for you.*

I recognize that conveying deep topics is challenging for any writer. The first time I read Eckhart Tolle's *A New Earth*, I felt uneducated. Don't get me wrong, Mr. Tolle is brilliant and an excellent teacher, but it was as if I was reading a different language or had picked up a book in the middle of a series and missed the earlier books. I do not want you to have that same experience while reading this material.

Some of this information is deep. To support each person's experience, and to provide definitions for terms and names you might not be familiar with, I created an extensive glossary at the back of this book and online at my website (alexmarcoux. com/ascension-glossary). We are all on different paths, and I don't want to lose anyone.

Since 2011, I have been on a path learning about what this book introduces as "Pure Autism." Who are the Pure Autists, and what do they have to do with humanity's spiritual evolution? To simplify, let's just say they are higher spiritual beings. I've devoted the past decade to learning from them, studying, and writing books like *The Unsuspected Heroes* and *Destination New Earth*.

Over the years, I've sensed that some spiritual teachers, particularly those asking to be followed, were not authentic. Yet, I've never felt inauthenticity with the Autists. They've never asked to be followed nor demanded anything from anyone.

They are here serving us and asking much of their families and caregivers to support them while doing their work, all because they love us.

I used fiction to communicate their stories in *The Unsuspected Heroes*. I chose that path because it felt safer to reveal what I'd learned in a novel. This book is nonfiction. However, as the novel reads "out of this world," so will *Destination New Earth* because the *truth is unbelievable*. There is no doubt that some readers will dub this book blasphemous. Others will cry, "Conspiracy theory!"

This information is not exactly warm and fuzzy. Some of it is downright controversial. But it is time to make it known to humanity. *Destination New Earth* will resonate with some, while others will be challenged by it. Although it is not yet clear where you will fit, I ask that you read this with an open heart and mind. That is your job. My job is to convey the information that resonates as Truth.

Deep gratitude for you and all that you do,
Alex Marcoux

PART I

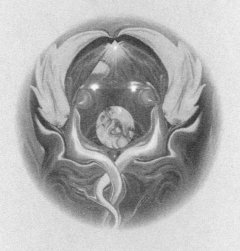

In the Beginning

CHAPTER 1:

Truth with a Capital "T"

When more and more people resonate by living their Truth, individually, they are a note. Collectively they are a symphony.
—Cerian

EVER SINCE I CAN REMEMBER, I have searched for Truth. No, that capital "T" on Truth is not a typo. I am not referring to the truth as something factual or a deeply held belief. What I mean is that I have searched for the Truth about God, the meaning of life, who we are, and why we are here.

As a fourth-grader, I remember Sister Clara asking me to stand before my classmates and unexpectedly drilling me with questions regarding religion. This oral examination was the first my teacher had given our class, so I was a bit surprised and nervous. With each correct answer to her questions, however, my confidence grew. Then she asked, "Out of all the apostles, who betrayed Jesus?"

"Peter," I said.

"That is wrong," smiling, almost taking delight in my error.

"Peter denied Jesus Christ three times," I squeaked out. "Judas was Jesus's loyal friend."

"Peter indeed denied Christ, but Judas betrayed him by handing him over to the authorities for some coins."

We had a few other words; then, I heard something that has never left me. Sister Clara called me a "dumb Marcoux." Those two words stayed with me, and I somehow pledged to prove her wrong.

I share that story not to mar your impression of the nun but to thank her publicly. Undoubtedly, being labeled "dumb" motivated me to prove otherwise to protect my father's name. More importantly, it steered me on a path to search for many Truths lost to humanity.

I grew up Roman Catholic. Our family was deep-rooted in its traditions; I even had an aunt who was a nun and an uncle who was a priest. My parents expected that I follow the faith. As a young girl, I thought about being a priest but learned I couldn't because I was the wrong sex. The message from this blatant sexual discrimination was that only men were good enough to receive the sacrament of ordination, or holy orders. That was something that never felt right with me.

When one of my older cousins married a Jewish man, my uncle, the priest, forbade the family to attend my cousin's wedding. The family became estranged over this incident for decades, and healing did not begin until my uncle passed away.

My experiences told me that the Church holds great control over people and families. When I divorced my husband in my early twenties, the Church's rules prevented me from participating in the sacrament of Holy Communion during mass. Then, it turned its back on me once again when I chose the companionship of a same-sex partner.

When researching one of my earlier novels, I dove into the Old Testament and was horrified that Jehovah hardened the people's hearts so they would resist Him—so He could slaughter them (Joshua 6, 10; Exodus 10). I did not recall this information being part of my CCD (Confraternity of Christian Doctrine) education when I was in high school.

As an adult, I broached the subject with my mother, trying to understand how she could follow a faith with such a God. She said she hadn't read the Bible, as they were discouraged to do so but were encouraged to follow on blind faith and the Church's interpretations provided to the congregants.

The Church has many secrets, and some are coming to light, like in 1969 after the Second Vatican Council when it *quietly* announced that Mary Magdalene was no longer the whore in the New Testament, but that's the tip of the iceberg.

I am not anti-Catholic; in fact, I am grateful that I grew up in the Church. It provided a rich foundation of information, instilled a curiosity within me, and indirectly encouraged that I ask questions. Some answers to my questions provide opportunities for healing humanity, which has led me to write this book.

SYNCHRONICITIES AND THE ROSE

Throughout my life, synchronicities, meaningful coincidences have guided me. Sometimes I get the messages right away, while other times, it can take years for the lightbulb to go off, and then, after the fact, I know the sign's meaning.

The first synchronicities I recall were when I was in my twenties and involved the rose. At the time, plentiful appearances or signs of the rose became so mysterious that I ended up getting two tattoos of a rose when it wasn't exactly fashionable for women to get tattoos.

Decades later, while searching for Truth, I learned that the rose and lily symbolize Mary Magdalene or the Magdalenes (a group of Essenes that included Mary Magdalene, Yeshua (Jesus), Mother Mary, Anna, and many others). Only recently, it hit me that my grandmother on my mother's side was Lillia LaFleur (meaning "lily the flower"), and my paternal grandmother's maiden name was Derosier, meaning "from the rose bushes." Could the Universe have been telling me all along to seek the Truth in the Magdalene line?

In any case, my quest for Truth has been lifelong, and many of my lessons and discoveries have made their way into earlier novels and my spiritual self-help book, *Lifesigns: Tapping the Power of Synchronicity, Serendipity and Miracles.*

THE UNSUSPECTED HEROES

In 2011, I was connected with Gayle Lee and Lyrica Marquez through an odd referral. They hired me to help them move their book, *AWEtizm: A Hidden Key to Our Spiritual Magnificence*, into the marketplace. To say that this interaction changed my life is an understatement. The two women welcomed me into their world, one of the sacred mysteries involving autism. As our friendship grew, I was astonished by their story. When their book failed to get the messages out into the mainstream, they asked me to write their story.

After denying them once, when they asked a second time, I agreed to write a novel inspired by their lives and the lives of other autistics I had the honor of meeting. Their story is so out of this world, I thought, *Why not write it as fiction?* Maybe then their truth would be less threatening.

That book is *The Unsuspected Heroes*, the story of a young autistic girl who is an Ascended Master reincarnated with autism. Her autism is her chosen disguise to hide from dark forces so that the Autists can work without interference to do their part in the planetary ascension. While that book is visionary fiction, it is about the Autists' work on the planet.

For those unfamiliar with the term, the Ascended Masters are beings who ascended to the higher realms (dimensions) in earlier lifetimes. There are many Masters, but we are often only familiar with Jesus, Mother Mary, Buddha, Anna, St. Germaine, and St. Francis in our western world. The simple truth, however, is that there are many others. And many Masters have chosen to return to our planet to assist in what's happening as we face humanity's spiritual evolution.

At one point in my life, I attended an introductory intuition training workshop and saw substantial growth in my creativity. Because of this, I completed the Association for Research and Enlightenment (A.R.E.) Edgar Cayce Institute for Intuitive Studies Wayshower's program.

During this intuition and psychic training, I had several professional psychic readings as part of the courses, and a couple of readings revealed some interesting information. One psychic said I would have access to the Akashic records one day and write books that would reveal Truths to heal conscious-nesses. The Akashic records are a compilation of all past, pres-ent, and future thoughts, events, emotions, and intentions of all lifeforms encoded in the ethers. Another psychic called me a healer, not a "hands-on" type healer but one who would heal on a planetary level.

While these comments were memorable, they never hit home with me until recently. Two of the contributors to this book are Connie and her son, Daniel. Daniel is one of the autistics who inspired *The Unsuspected Heroes*. When I first met Connie and her family, there was an instant trust between us. I recall sharing some things about myself that I hadn't shared with anyone. I am usually very private, so this was out of character.

Likewise, as I became more involved with researching and writing *The Unsuspected Heroes*, my interactions with Connie, her husband, and Daniel increased. During this early "getting to know you" period, the family shared many personal and private stories with me. At some point, I asked why they trusted me with their information. Connie turned to Daniel and asked him why they felt so comfortable sharing with me.

Daniel, an Ethereal Autist who works in the ethers with energies, communicates through facilitated communication. He answered, "Because she is the Medicine Woman."

Facilitated communication (FC) is a supported typing method that helps some nonspeaking autistics communicate. Because many autistics do not fully physically embody, and most of their essence remains in the higher dimensions, they are not always in control of their bodies, making simple typing difficult. In FC, a facilitator holds and stabilizes the autistic's wrist, hand, or arm so that the autistic types. The facilitator *does not* guide the autistic but provides slight resistance so that the autistic points to the keys with more accuracy.

I knew it was imperative to get the Ethereal Autists' story into the world. But it was only recently, during the launch of *The Unsuspected Heroes*, that I connected Daniel calling me the Medicine Woman with the earlier psychic readings about accessing the Akashic records and writing books revealing Truths to heal the planet. I now know it is the Ethereal Autists who have access to the Akashic records, and it is my honor to share the information with the world in the hopes that it heals the planet.

Historically, books communicating truths or information that *certain* parties did not want to have shared were confiscated and burned to prevent the material from being read. These acts occurred in our ancient past, Middle Ages, and happen even today. It is censorship. Another form of control not often discussed is algorithmic censorship.

Algorithms control what we can find on the internet. Every day we search our computers or phones with search engines like Google, Bing, or Yahoo. And we search for products and books with search engines like Amazon, the largest online e-commerce retailer.

As an SEO specialist during my daytime job, I know that people manipulate algorithms, and the algorithms change all the time. The algorithms control which products rank, in other words, which products you see when you search for something. Some books can be published and listed correctly with appropriate SEO factors yet never rank.

You found this book somehow, and I am incredibly grateful for your attention to this material. I ask a favor, however. If you find this material interesting and helpful on your ascension journey, would you please share the information with those you know who would benefit from it? This information is important and needs to be understood. I trust people to spread the news, not computer-implementable instructions.

I do not want anyone to get the impression that I am asking you to follow us. If this information resonates and you are eager to learn more, I hope you read the visionary fiction books, beginning with *The Unsuspected Heroes*, as they are full of insights. I will continue that series, sharing truths in fiction as more is revealed to me. More importantly, I hope this book opens you to *your* Truth. If you have not opened that door to your Christic Consciousness, I invite you not to follow but join us on this journey, destination New Earth.

CHAPTER 2:

The Parties Coming Together

It doesn't matter how slow you go,
so long as you do not stop!
—Confucius

OVER TWENTY YEARS AGO, I was at a conference with a friend, and she was walking me to my hotel room. While we walked the hallway, my friend's voice changed, and she started saying things that didn't make sense to me.

She repeatedly said, "Alex, you are special. You need to get moving."

I always cringe at the word "special." I've always believed that either no one is special or everyone is special. But I let that part pass and asked, "Why do I have to get moving?"

"Because we need to raise the consciousness of the planet!" she said seriously.

I had no idea what she was saying. After the conference, I sent her a note reminding her of our conversation and asked what she meant by raising the planet's consciousness. She was clueless and did not remember that part of our conversation.

How could she not? The chat was so unusual and stayed with me. I didn't understand what she meant.

When I shared this story with Connie, she reminded me that Autists "talk" through other people to deliver messages. She indicated that she was aware that Daniel had done this a few times. Could it have been an Ethereal Autist? When I look back, I realize it wasn't the first time I received messages in this manner.

Today, the phrase "raise the consciousness of the planet" seems so popular, so much so that it has become a cliché and lost meaning. But I don't want to assume you know what it means.

There is a change occurring on our planet.

That change impacts all of us, and all of us affect the change.

Humankind has a crucial role in this change.

That change is a planetary shift in consciousness.

Consciousness is the awareness of the self, thoughts, beliefs, feelings of the world around us. There is much discussion in the various texts about what it means to raise consciousness. Can we consider for a moment that raising consciousness is to elevate our vibration of who we are from an energetic perspective?

Everything is energy. Energy vibrates and oscillates at a specific speed and frequency. Frequency is the rate at which the energy vibrates. Everything, including humans, has a vibrational frequency. The higher the vibrational frequency, the greater one experiences peace, joy, and clarity. As our frequency rises, we can shift our awareness of ourselves to new levels.

The shift in consciousness is known by other names, like planetary ascension, the paradigm shift, humanity's spiritual evolution, but my favorite is the New Earth. There are books by many others on the New Earth, from religious leaders, philosophers, academics, and those with more letters after their names than me. So, what does this book provide that makes it unique? Hang on.

The first Autist to reach out to me was Lyrica Marquez, who communicates with her mother through facilitated communication. This mother and daughter communication evolved over decades and eventually integrated telepathy with supported typing. Telepathy is communicating through extrasensory means or from one mind to another. Some may refer to it as mind reading.

Daniel only began using the typing process in 2014, so he types slower than Lyrica, who is about twenty years older. After I started working on *The Unsuspected Heroes*, I learned that Daniel would rate books for accuracy. The highest grade for a book I remember him giving at the time was an eight, meaning 80 percent of the information in that book was accurate. That book was *Anna, Grandmother of Jesus* by Claire Heartsong. When Daniel's mother, Connie, sat down to read Heartsong's text aloud so that Daniel could hear, he typed, "I know this story already but love hearing it again." At the time, this threw Connie since she had never read the story to him.

I began researching and writing *The Unsuspected Heroes* in 2014. I was on a mission to seek Truths and reveal them in a less threatening way than nonfiction. I wanted to plant seeds. With it, I started reading many books on spiritual evolution, God, creation, the soul, multidimensionality, aliens, and spiritual gurus throughout history. From these texts, I'd pose questions to Daniel through Connie. Unfortunately, this process was long and tedious. My only way to Daniel was through his mother. With nearly a thousand miles separating us and telepathy not being my strength, I soon realized that writing *The Unsuspected Heroes* would take years.

ENTER SHAUNA KALICKI, THE CHANNEL

In 2016, while in Colorado preparing for a Peru adventure, I went through the Munay Ki shamanic initiation rites. One of the women performing the rituals was Shauna Kalicki. After one ceremony, Shauna approached me and shared that she sensed a powerful male presence around me while performing an initiation. Later, she shared that it was Archangel Metatron.

Before that trip to Peru, my dear friend Lyrica had entered hospice because her body was shutting down. Shauna had made a last-minute decision to join the group I was traveling with, and while in Peru, we engaged in many conversations. During those one-on-one discussions, I shared that I was writing books revealing how Autists work selflessly behind the scenes on humanity's spiritual evolution. In a quiet moment on Machu Picchu, I asked Shauna if she sensed that Lyrica would transition soon.

She tuned in and heard a resounding, "No! She's not going to pass."

As I write this, Lyrica has not transitioned. However, she has teetered between life and death throughout her embodiment and ascension process on more than one occasion. She writes about her experiences in her 2021 book, *Lyrica's Journey of Ascension.*

When I returned from my Peru adventure, I agreed to reconnect with Shauna to discuss our trip experiences. After continuing our conversations, I suspected that Shauna had a past life connection with Daniel. She shared that she was an apprentice of a well-known mythic figure that I knew was Daniel in a past life. I shared the information with Daniel, who confirmed that he knew Shauna and called her Rasew. He even typed a message, instructing his mother to send Shauna a sacred oil his father had created. While called Sophia Oil, Daniel later revealed in a telepathic message, "Perhaps another name would be Mary's oil or Magdalene oil, not suggesting that the name be changed ... perhaps an alignment to this idea."

When Connie mailed the oil to Shauna, Daniel typed, "Sacred oil on the way to the Gatekeeper," creating even more mystery to the connection between Daniel and my new friend.

For some reason, I am a connector. I see this now; throughout my life, I have connected people. It became clear that Shauna had work to do with more than one member of our small group. She connected with Daniel and another Autist named Leilah, who had been quiet in our group for quite some time.

In an email, Shauna shared with a group of us her mystical experiences when using the Sophia Oil. She explained that she worked with Archangel Michael, St. Germaine, Lord Maitreya, and other Ascended Masters. That group included the parents of three Autists.

Shortly after receiving Shauna's email, Leilah's mother replied to the group with a note from Leilah. "Dear Shauna, I pray for your continued awakening. Please open your heart to me, and I will visit. I can help you. Love everlasting, Leilah."

Leilah came out of her shell and began sending Shauna emails through her mother. Shauna came on board, interested in exploring Truths I would reveal in *The Unsuspected Heroes* and its sequels. She demonstrated psychic abilities and picked up messages from Archangels. But our discovery took a substantial turn in 2018 when she and I were on a hike, and Shauna suddenly said, "Leilah is here."

Given that Leilah lived nearly two thousand miles away, and they had never met in person, I was a bit skeptical yet curious. At the time, I was researching *The Ra Material* (*The Law of One*) for *The Unsuspected Heroes* and had many questions. I knew these high vibrational Autists had the answers. "If you have Leilah's attention," I asked Shauna, "can she answer some questions on the Law of One?"

Leilah answered a series of questions through Shauna, and then I asked if Leilah would help us get information for our books. She agreed, with the caveat that Daniel would need to verify the information that we received and that codenames were to be used to assure that Shauna was speaking with her (Leilah) and that I, for some unknown reason, be present.

Before I considered this, I needed to confirm that Shauna had spoken with Leilah. Shortly after our hike, I wrote to Leilah's mother and said that her daughter showed up to Shauna psychically. I asked if she could verify this with Leilah.

Very quickly, I received an email back.

Hi Alex,

I just asked Leilah if she knew who emailed me yesterday, and she typed, "I talked to Shauna on Sunday, and she understood me." She didn't want to add more, but it seems like they made a connection!

Our fiction series was now moving and shaking! With the Autist talking telepathically to Shauna, this psychic communication saved us much time. We began sessions where Shauna would go into a meditative trance, and I would ask questions and record the sessions. Connie would transcribe the sessions and ask Daniel for verifications.

Shortly after Shauna began conversing with the Autists, mostly Leilah and Daniel, though Lyrica came in from time to time, Shauna began channeling messages from Archangels and Ascended Masters, including Archangel Michael, Metatron, Anna, the grandmother of Jesus, Joachim, Mother Mary, Jesus, Mary Magdalene, and others. These communications went on until October 2018, and then one day in a channeling session, a voice came through and said, "This is Cerian."

We learned that Cerian is a conscious, sentient, collective expression of an energetic field or vibrational pattern of beings from the sixteenth dimension. It is a collective consciousness speaking through one voice, similar in scope to *The Ra Material: Law of One*. "*I am Ra*" is a sixth-dimension collective expression channeled by Carla Rueckert in the 1980s.

Why Cerian came to the party also proved to be interesting.

CHAPTER 3:

Who Is Rasew?

*This book is about the awakening of the here
and now rather than the future state.*
—Daniel

WHEN SHAUNA CAME INTO THE FOLD, Daniel never
called her by her name. Instead, he has always called her Rasew
(sounds like RAZU). For the longest time, we assumed that it
went back to a past life. Although we are still not clear, it may
go back to Cerian. After Cerian made its entry, we had a channeling and brought in Daniel.

Daniel shared in that channeling, "Rasew and I share a
higher aspect. It is Cerian. It is easier for the channel, Rasew, to
access Cerian. Sometimes I may be busy in an alternate reality
known as 'Daniel,' but my higher self and Rasew's higher self
can tap into each other much more readily than if we call in

myself or if we ask Rasew to call in herself and her higher self to connect with me."

Think of the higher self as the soul. The soul is multidimensional and has multiple experiences in various dimensions at the same time. Both Shauna and Daniel have an existence as an aspect of Cerian, an energetic pattern within the sixteenth dimension. During our channelings, it was easier for Shauna to connect with Cerian than for her to link up with Rasew to get a hold of Daniel.

When Shauna channels Daniel, he shows us time and space, and individuality; in other words, Daniel is there. When channeling Cerian, another aspect of Daniel and Shauna, they are both there. It is a shared consciousness and experience, and they can both readily tap into it.

After explaining it, Daniel said, "This is why we would suggest using Cerian; it is a good channel."

OUR ROLES FOR THIS BOOK

This book is nonfiction. It shares *what* the New Earth is now, not in the future, but on our planet *today*.

Our group took the gathering of the information and writing of this book seriously. We started with Connie, Shauna, and me, and then Daniel quickly jumped in—in many different ways.

Connie and I generated questions, guiding where the book would go. Shauna provided the foundation of the content through channeling sessions in which I interviewed her. During the information gathering, Shauna connected primarily with Cerian, Mother Mary, and Daniel. Connie transcribed the channelings and sought accuracy ratings from Daniel. Throughout this process, Connie and I also intuitively discerned the information. Daniel provided not only ratings but encouraged direction on future channelings and provided comments. Those comments are shared in this book with a `different font to demonstrate it was through facilitated communications.` In comparison, dialogue from Daniel is mainly from a channeling session (unless noted).

Once the channeling sessions were complete and transcribed, I took the highly-rated content and wrote the book using inner guidance. As you will see, Connie provided other stories as well.

Given that my education was in science, I applied scientific principles to ensure that we did not bias the channel or the generated information. Shauna did not know the book's subject matter or the questions until I asked her during the sessions. She also was not privy to the transcripts or recordings until the content was complete.

We all took great care to gather this information and deliver it in a way that may open a newcomer to spiritual concepts yet provide unique content to satisfy those who have been on the path for years. As noted earlier, we have included an extensive glossary at the back of this book to support your understanding and journey.

WHAT IS CHANNELING?

A medium is a specific type of psychic who mediates communication between individuals and spirits or other-dimensional entities. This process of communication is known as channeling. For quite some time, Shauna's communication was psychic, where she would relay what she saw, felt, and heard.

In 2018, a small group, including Shauna and me, went to Chaco Canyon to perform a summer solstice ceremony. Shortly after that ritual, Shauna surprised me when she entered a trancelike state during a session, and Mother Mary spoke through her.

Some mediums retain awareness of the events, whereas a trance medium generally goes into a trance and does not retain an understanding of the discussion. As I understand it, Shauna can come out of a session with some awareness of the session, but the details generally escape her.

After Cerian emerged in late 2018, most of the information from our sessions came from this sixteenth-dimensional collective. My experience interviewing Shauna for *this* book was different from our earlier work together. For this book, most of the material came from channeling Daniel, though Cerian, Mother Mary, and other entities would observe and join in at times.

Perhaps Daniel's interest was because his mother, Connie, took a pivotal role in transcribing the sessions. Then, of course, she'd ask him to verify the information. I think it goes deeper than that, however. I believe the information contained herein needs to come out and is important for humanity's contribution in bringing the New Earth awareness to a new level. I learned how critical Daniel's role was in verifying the material when a trickster entity hijacked one session.

CHANNELING A TRICKSTER

When Cerian and Daniel came in during one session, another entity, who claimed to be an aspect of Daniel, stole the show. Shauna later shared what she had been experiencing during the channeling. In the beginning, Daniel worked on Shauna's third eye. With a finger, he spiraled her forehead, and suddenly Shauna saw in much more vivid detail and proceeded to describe this newcomer with great clarity. The entity claimed to be an angel named Daveed.

I asked the first question and knew it wasn't Daniel. Shauna's mannerisms, speech, and the length of the answers were different. When Daniel speaks, Shauna's head frequently oscillates or swings back and forth at a steady speed. His answers are usually very concise. When Cerian speaks, it uses the first-person plural pronoun "we," and the information is typically lengthier than Daniel. The others also have different descriptors.

After a lengthy opening statement, I knew Shauna wasn't channeling Daniel. "Who's speaking?" I asked.

"This is Daveed."

Daveed introduced himself as an angelic aspect of Daniel. After the channeling, Shauna explained that this newcomer would speak, and Daniel would pop in, replacing Daveed. This back-and-forth morphing continued throughout the channeling.

Typically, after a channeling session, I send the audio file to Connie and wait for the transcription. The morning after this session, though, I messaged Connie to ask Daniel if an aspect of him claiming to be an angel came into the channeling.

His response was, "No. It was a trickster. Be careful."

Daniel instructed Connie not to listen to the channeling, adding that the information was not for our book.

I share this to show how vital Daniel's role became in this project. Other entities claiming to work for the light can take over channeling sessions even after we've called in protection and invoked only the highest and best good. There is some logic to their appearance, in that the tricksters provide the "highest and best good" for themselves. Daniel is a safeguard to ensure other entities do not taint the information shared.

DANIEL'S COMMENTS ON THIS BOOK

In one channeling, Daniel wanted to share information about this book, and I share it here. The words in quotes are Daniel's messages.

"Energetically, we see lights shining around the books coming out. This book is about the Autists and the *awakening of the here and now* rather than the future state."

There is much information published about the New Earth. Many of these books suggest that an event will occur, and then we'll be on the New Earth. They speak more to the future. We are here to tell you that the New Earth is here now.

"The book is about humanity's accountability to themselves and not pushing it out to somebody else to fix it."

Each of us is responsible for our awakening, and we can't expect a savior to come in and save us.

"The Autist Collective works very closely with humankind, but humankind must step up and take accountability for what they have created and what they choose to create."

We are all creators of our reality. If we don't like what we see, it's our responsibility to own that we've created it and fix it.

"The Autist Collective is here to assist, but our work alone, without humanity being accountable for its sovereignty, will not matter if humanity does not take the needed steps to look at themselves and do the work."

Doesn't this sound like you can lead a horse to water, but you can't make them drink? The Autist Collective is a group of Ethereal Autists who work around the planet to awaken humanity, but humanity has to make the choice.

"Humanity is accountable for its sovereignty. It is your birthright."

You are a sovereign being. Live your life as *you* will. You are a supreme being, but not to any other. You are unique and have a right to individuality, free of the illusion that you are separate from Source. Accept ownership of your entire self, including your shadows.

"We see that these books can be a portal for many, and you have behind you the Autists, not only of planet Earth but of various realms, galaxies, universes that are here to assist with this. Know this, be aware of this, and continue to work on this. It is important!"

Consider that this book is a doorway or a bridge to understanding a new perspective. Be open to the miracles it will ignite within.

PART II

What Is the New Earth?

CHAPTER 4:

Defining the New Earth

*It is humanity's awareness of Itself
that shifts into the New Earth.*
—Mother Mary

OVER THE LAST COUPLE OF DECADES, I've heard many different theories about what *will* happen in the shift or planetary ascension. Some speculate that the Earth will split into two dimensions: our current third dimension (3D) and the fifth dimension (5D). Another theory is that some will ascend to the heavens while others will be *left behind*. Some suggest that those remaining behind will end in apocalyptic destruction while those climbing to the higher realms will live in peace and unconditional love without dualities.

This shift is truly a spiritual evolution that has been in the making for eons. *The Ra Material: Law of One* revealed there are opportunities for ascension every twenty-six thousand years, though they refer to it as "harvests," and we are currently in that time of harvest. In this case, we would ascend from third density to fourth density, assuming we have polarized toward one pole or another, the poles being "service to others" or "service to self."

Then, of course, the Bible talks about the New Heavens and New Earth as the eternal dwelling place for those believing in Jesus and those who are righteous. According to the Bible, there will be no more sin, suffering, or death in this place.

I've mentioned that this shift has many names: the ascension, the awakening, the paradigm shift, shift in consciousness, even spiritual evolution. It is essentially humankind's evolution from the third dimension to the fifth dimension or the New Earth. **This book is not about what will happen; it is about what *is* happening now.**

If you are a newcomer to the spiritual path, welcome. There is no doubt that this information will stretch you. If you've been on the spiritual path for some time, you may find portions of this book to be elementary. However, I encourage you to bear with me, as I guarantee you will discover unique information.

WHAT IS THE DEFINITION OF THE NEW EARTH?

One of the first questions I asked during a channeling was, "Can you define the New Earth?"

At the time, Shauna was channeling Mother Mary, the mother of Jesus. Her response was very complicated, and after the channeling, Daniel deemed it highly accurate.

"The New Earth is a shared experience by many," Mother Mary began, "an expression that humanity agrees to, which is coherence, meaning it matches the vibrational patterns of the Earth's growth and all within it. And that is being in sync or within resonance or harmonic with it, rather than separate from it."

I share this passage not to risk losing you in this early chapter. I quickly learned that I would need to deconstruct much of the content because I want it to be understood by all (even me, and I write that with a grin). I want to stretch your muscles, for this book is about growth, but I don't want to lose you on the journey's threshold.

Humanity agreed to experience this shift occurring at the planetary level, meaning that Mother Gaia, Earth, is shifting along with all on and within it. The *experience* of coherence, of being in sync with the Earth's growth, is the New Earth. It is a new expression for humankind.

Many consider the fifth dimension the New Earth's realm, while Earth's is the third. According to Maureen St. Germain, author of *Waking Up in 5D*, it is not a whole number, meaning

3.0, and if we were to round to the nearest whole number, Earth would be closer to the fourth dimension (4D). There are many dimensions and many levels between each dimension. However, for simplicity, we will occasionally refer within this book to our physical Earth experience as the third dimension and the New Earth experience as the fifth dimension or 5D consciousness.

Mother Mary shared that the fifth-dimensional level is closer to the flow of the Universe's natural laws, meaning "ease and grace" or "flow." There are natural rhythms within the Universe, and when humanity is one with this natural rhythm, this fifth dimension, humankind evolves to the next level and experiences the New Earth.

She explained, "The human form *must* be able to raise its vibrational patterns (to experience the ascension). As you begin to vibrate at a higher level, new frequencies, or sounds, can be experienced. The range expands what human consciousness has been aware of before."

Remember that everything is energy, and to ascend the dimensions, we must raise our vibrational pattern or frequency.

Have you ever, on occasion, experienced high-pitched sounds in your ears? The medical community often diagnoses tinnitus for such experiences. I am not suggesting that the condition doesn't exist. I am, however, asking that you consider another possibility. Perhaps those high-pitched sounds are your way of experiencing new frequencies.

Given that everything is energy and has a specific vibrational pattern and frequency, the New Earth matches the vibrational patterns of the Earth's growth and all within it, meaning that Gaia and all are part of the living Earth are in sync or within resonance (harmonic) rather than separate. Gaia is evolving along with all within the Earth: plants, animals, the elemental kingdom, even a portion of humans.

Mother Mary finished answering my question by saying something that repeats throughout our dialogues, "The New Earth already exists. It is just that humanity has not been able to access it."

When asking Daniel if Mother Mary's response was accurate, he gave the passage a high rating, then typed, "All of this is true, but there is more beyond infinity."

This book will explore many Truths and convey them to educate, enlighten, and activate the reader to bring awareness to the emerging New Earth.

NEW HEAVENS AND NEW EARTH

If you are a biblical scholar, you may be familiar with the passages discussing the New Heavens and New Earth. These mentions are in the books of Isaiah, 2 Peter, and Revelation. They describe it as the final state of redeemed humanity and the world to come.

According to Mother Mary, the New Earth is *not* a final state of redemption for humanity. "Humans are fractals of

Source Energy. There are numerous levels between humanity and Source, and until one merges with Source, returning home, one is constantly redeemed."

WHAT IS SOURCE ENERGY?

You can think of Source Energy as God. It is the source from which all things come. A fractal is a complex energetic pattern that is never-ending. Imagine a glass pane consisting of similar repeating patterns throughout the glass. Then picture taking a hammer and shattering it into countless pieces. All pieces of that glass contain the self-similar blueprint of the original pane at different levels. The shards of glass are essentially step-down versions of the pane.

Humans are step-down versions of Source Energy or, using slightly different words, unique expressions of God.

As an expression of Source Energy, you are here to experience. You are here to explore, make mistakes, build, erase, and start over again with new awareness at the end of your physical existence. That is creation. Mother Mary said, "You are on a path and journey, and when the New Earth is complete, there will be other opportunities, expeditions, expressions, and redemptions."

There are many levels between the New Earth and our end destination, returning to Source. Contrary to the biblical references suggesting the New Earth is the final state of redemption, you are constantly redeemed until you return to the Source of creation.

The New Earth is being experienced and shared by many now. You agreed to participate in this experience as a unified whole. Of course, you don't remember this, and that is the journey, one of awakening and remembering and claiming your sovereignty, which was hidden from humanity eons ago. Who hid it?

Fasten your seatbelt!

CHAPTER 5:

The Hundredth Monkey Effect and the Event

*The New Earth is formed, yet it is a probabil-
ity and possibility, and humanity plays a large
role in bringing it into humanity's awareness.*
—Mother Mary

THE NEW EARTH IS HERE. Some people perceive it, and
more will in time. How long it will take is unclear and depends
on how fast humanity wakes up. As more and more experience
the New Earth, and once a specific percent of the population, a
critical mass, perceives it, there will be a significant awakening.

Currently, the majority of humanity is experiencing the fifth-dimension energy light. It is in our subconscious, though, and we don't quite know what it is yet. Consider this fifth-dimension energy light as a knowing or knowledge coming to humanity to assist us in our awakening.

Other people suggest that an event will occur in the future that will take us to the New Earth. Yet, we know the New Earth is here already. I like to think of this event as reaching critical mass, the hundredth monkey effect that will create rapid awareness of the New Earth among humanity.

THE MYTH

One challenge to uncovering many Truths is that humanity has not been introduced to concepts to explain them. Without understanding a concept, there is no language to describe it. When working with channeled information, this is an ongoing obstacle. One message I received from an Autist early on was to forget everything I've ever learned. I'm not asking that you do this. I am asking you to consider suspending belief because many of the concepts within this text will challenge your current understanding.

Throughout history, people told myths when words and concepts did not exist to explain Truths. These tales were for bringing in knowledge. A myth provides a way to convey profound Truths when language fails to describe them. At the heart of most legends, there are Truths. What if you had to explain what Bluetooth wireless technology was to someone in the Middle Ages? There is a vocabulary for this technology in the twenty-first century but go back 1,500 years. How would you explain it? You'd tell a myth.

To add to this, Daniel said during one channeling that some questions have no answers. "They are unanswerable because there are infinite possibilities. There is always an unknown component all the time. It is part of the game."

The game? I'll get to that.

Daniel's statement sure puts a different perspective on what the Greek philosopher Heraclitus said: "Change is the only constant." When I asked questions of the channel during the creation of this book, the responses at times included the phrases *probability* and *possibility*. This is an indication that we are in flux. Life is fluid and ever-changing. If life is a moving target, we can only share that things are either probable, meaning likely to happen or be true, or possible, a chance that something will happen or be true.

Myths, fables, folktales, and legends have shared knowledge throughout time. Even much of our ancient sacred texts include myths. Given that New Heavens and New Earth are in the Bible, I asked Mother Mary in a channeling, "Is the New Earth a myth?"

"Humanity can right now, this very moment, live in the New Earth if they understand their ability to shift their perception," Mother Mary said. "We use that as a singularity, meaning humanity as a singular focus, but it does not happen as a singular focus. With humanity, it starts with every individual. Is it a myth? In many respects, yes!"

The emergence of the New Earth starts with every person. As more and more perceive and experience the New Earth, the awareness of it increases. It is not up to one individual or a savior to trigger the New Earth emergence. Once a critical number of humans (the hundredth monkey effect) perceive the New Earth, it will emerge for those on an ascension path or those *choosing* to experience it.

"The New Earth is humanity waking unto Itself." It will still take much time in the third, fourth, and fifth dimensions. "It is not an immediate shift, it could be, but our experience is that typically it is not."

The New Earth is here, has *always* been here, and isn't new. Yet, most do not experience it. Humanity currently wants to experience the end result rather than the New Earth's progression and expansion. "It is humanity's *awareness of Itself* that shifts into the New Earth."

As humans, we want instant gratification. We want to see the New Earth in all its glory rather than the small brilliant manifestations. Understand that giving or receiving simple acts of kindness, increased intuition, increased psychic activity, instantaneous manifestations, Mandela effects (which we talk about in Chapter 22: Multidimensionality 101), synchronicities, unexplained occurrences, or miracles are all New Earth manifestations. All are baby steps in perceiving the New Earth.

Be grateful for the baby steps and welcome them with joy, gratitude, and expectation.

By celebrating the awe in life, you will see more and more extraordinary situations emerge. You will realize that *you* created them. You are the divine creator of your reality, and this awareness shifts you into the New Earth—but it does not come from outside of you.

Mother Mary shared, "The New Earth is formed, yet it is a probability and possibility, and humanity plays a large role in bringing it into humanity's awareness."

While the New Earth is here, and humanity's experience of it is likely, it isn't a done deal. Meaning humanity has some work to do. It is up to humankind to access it, awaken, and eventually trigger the population to experience it.

The shift to the fifth dimension, to New Earth, is part of a plan that has been in the making for ages. "It is part of the evolution of both Gaia and humanity," Mother Mary shared. "It is emerging and will continue to emerge even as the systems fall apart."

Humanity's systems are currently failing. As we ascend from the third to the fourth to the fifth dimension, most will experience fluctuations up and down the dimensions. Humanity agreed to participate and play within this paradigm shift, and it is occurring now.

THE 144,000

There are messages within numbers and, indeed, the numbers 144,000 and 144. The Bible and other sacred texts discuss the number 144,000, and its interpretations have made their way into many faiths, organized religions, and New Age beliefs.

The Jehovah's Witnesses believe that only 144,000 Christians will ascend to heaven, becoming immortal to rule with Jesus.

New Age-like beliefs suggest that based on the Bible and *The Emerald Tablet,* 144,000 Lightworkers will walk the planet during the end of times, or the Kali Yuga, which is the present age. These Lightworkers will lift the veil of consciousness and show the way to the New Earth.

When I asked Daniel about the references to 144,000 in the texts, he implied that it has nothing to do with the number of people, as there are many more than 144,000 working on shifting the consciousness. He did type a message about it, however.

"There is an energy to everything, and 144 is a divine number. When it is time for a number to come forward and be prominent like this number, be open to its divinity, it is a sign of something converging. When these numbers come up, you can take this as a sign of convergence. Think

```
bigger. Sometimes numerology can be
too detailed. Think bigger about the
numbers, but don't overthink. Just
feel into the energy of the numbers,
similar as you do for 11:11. All
numbers are divine. Open up to the
mystery of what that is."
```

Daniel's message seemed personal. We had never discussed numerology before, and I had never shared that 144 or 1111 were frequent synchronicities in my life. From my exploration of numbers, I know there are various meanings for 1111 or 11:11. An 11:11 can be an indication that one is on the right path and to remain aware. It can signify intuition and enlightenment. Also, the coming together of the two master numbers (11) can also indicate a sacred union of soulmates or twin souls.

Convergence is when things come together to form a whole. The 144 in numerology is a 9 (1+4+4=9) and a symbol of divine completeness. For Daniel to suggest that 144 is a sacred number and a sign of convergence, I immediately think of humanity as being on an evolutionary path of coherence with the Earth's vibration and growth rather than being separate from everything.

Could the 144 simply be to remind us that we are not separate from Source or God, and each is an expression of the One?

I also recognize that twin souls are reuniting at this time and can be considered a convergence. Twin souls (also known as twin flames or mirror souls) are two souls that were once one soul split into its yin and yang aspects. The purpose was to experience life differently and reunite with each other in unconditional love, impacting those around them energetically during this planetary shift.

The ascension has begun, and humanity is catching up energetically to the New Earth. That growth will be fast for some, while a snail's pace for others. Daniel explained, "The New Earth already exists in totality, and there is much beyond that as well. It allows humanity to register with the 5D energy light."

Some are detecting New Earth energy, while others do not. Some notice or register the 5D energy light, but they don't know what it is.

"The 5D energy is in humankind's subconscious; humanity is aware of it, humanity is expecting the energy, *but* they are expecting it to be brought from the outside in."

Perhaps this is a collective consciousness pattern for humanity? Is it possible that humankind expects a savior to save us? This is certainly in line with much of the current religious programming.

"Humanity is expecting something significant to transpire," Daniel continued. "They are expecting it to come from the outside. It must *always* come from within the consciousness of humanity."

People are aware that something is changing, but they aren't associating it with the New Earth. Acknowledge that the New Earth is in your subconscious and energetically within you. Know that *you are the one you have been waiting for,* and you will lead yourself to the New Earth.

CHAPTER 6:

Questions on the Fifth Dimension

*The fifth dimension is new vibrational energy
and frequency and is glorious to explore.*
—Daniel

DURING CHANNELING SESSIONS, I asked Daniel some questions about the fifth dimension. Here are some dialogues.

IS 5D A VIBRATIONAL FREQUENCY OF UNCONDITIONAL LOVE?

"Daniel, some people speculate that the fifth dimension is a vibrational frequency of unconditional love without fear and control. Is this true?" I asked.

"Not exactly," he said. "I would say that there is *less fear and control*. As we step our way up or down the dimensions, there will always be the concept of control. We become more *sovereign* in the fifth dimension, and as we begin to harmonize with that 5D energy, and that possibility and probability, it, too, is a sliding scale.

"Since the energy is learning to harmonize," he continued, "for most people, the dimensions will fluctuate. Some people will enter the fifth dimension by ascending 3D, 4D, to 5D. Others in the fourth dimension will climb to the fifth. Then others will return from the fifth dimension, perhaps descending from 5D, to 4D, and then 3D.

"Some will remain steady in the fifth dimension, and when that occurs, life will be more harmonious, love-filled, and sovereign. Others can step immediately into that energy, reflect life strongly within the 5D, and then shift up into the 6D and the 7D.

"People with the experience of stabilizing in the fifth dimension and moving upward toward 7D will harmonize differently than those escalating up and down energetically. There will be many energies and experiences within the 5D, just as there are currently in 3D."

Our dimensions fluctuate. We do not remain in any one dimension and shouldn't because we are here to experience and grow.

In another dialogue, I asked Cerian, the collective from the sixteenth dimension, about our 5D experiences. I suspected we would experience increased synchronicity, increased intuition, heightened senses, and divine guidance. I thought that things might be more in the flow, and there would be more joy and even bliss.

Cerian's response was, "All of this is available now and is too limiting. The singular self (the individual) in 5D will be able to guide their will, choices, and creations more accurately and will express who and what they are naturally while in the fifth dimension."

In 3D, we create our world, the good and the bad, though I prefer referring to the "bad" as "interesting." In 5D, we own our creations and become more responsible creators of our world. We also express more of our divinity as an expression of Source (God).

WILL THERE BE DUALITY IN 5D?

I want to put some definition on polarity and duality. One can think of polarity as simply opposites or contradictory sides of an opinion, aspect, or tendency. Examples would be light and dark, feminine and masculine, north and south, hot and cold. Polarity lacks what I call judgment. When judging situations that appear to be opposites, for example, good and bad, I call that duality. Duality creates contrast and potentially chaos, while polarity creates balance.

"Daniel, I read a book suggesting that there would be no duality in 5D, in the New Earth. Is that true?"

"There will be dualities, but not like what we experience in 3D," Daniel said. "Dualities will be for growth opportunities and *chosen* by the individual based on where they are in their growth and awareness of self and their relationship to energy as a whole. But it is *one* aspect within 5D. It is a choice. It does not have to be experienced."

There can be duality in 5D, though it is a choice. If the masses consciously agree to it, humanity may choose to carry duality forward, though not at the level we experience in the third dimension.

IS EARTH'S PLANETARY ASCENSION UNIQUE?

Many consider Gaia's planetary ascension an experiment and unique. When inquiring about this with Daniel, he offered the following.

The ascension we are currently facing "could potentially be the first time an entire planet, the awareness (meaning the consciousness and vibrational patterns of all species, sentient beings, or lifeforms within a planet), and a portion of humanity could evolve or raise the frequency."

Yes, Daniel did say a portion of humanity could evolve. That was another consistent message in the channeled material. Not everyone will ascend.

"Rather than having people rise in awareness and consciousness and collectively choose to leave the planet, it is feasible, and it is a probability that the full expression of Earth and the sentient beings within, on, and around Earth, as well as the human expression of consciousness, could also shift collectively."

Daniel suggests that the planetary ascension is probable. I found it interesting that he said, "within, on, and around Earth." Some beings live below ground. While this certainly is not part of our history, people sought refuge below ground during various periods of earlier cataclysms. One example is associated with the flood of Atlantis. Another mention is that the Sasquatch, or Bigfoot, are theorized to be beings who live below ground.

For the entire planet to ascend, Mother Mary said, "All aspects of Earth must vibrate collectively. Otherwise, Earth cannot harmonically move into the vibrational pattern of the New Earth."

There are levels of energy that humanity does not understand. Energy flows to, from, and through Earth and various kingdoms, including rocks, minerals, plants, animals, water, and more. All the energies must vibrate collectively to make this shift.

Gaia's ascension is unique and has drawn numerous galactic beings' attention because Earth's ascension impacts the entire universe.

WHAT ARE ASCENSION SYMPTOMS?

The following information was revealed by Cerian during a channeling when inquiring about the different energies (and frequencies) coming to the planet and how they impact our physical bodies. The content is paraphrased for simplification.

According to Cerian, new energies coming to the planet have different frequencies; some are lower, while most are much higher. Humanity is familiar with these energies from other timelines yet needs to remember and experience the more elevated, lighter energies to assimilate into the next expression.

For some, our bodies adjust as the energies come in. It is a gradual morphing for those who can absorb, modify, and change. With those who adapt to the fifth dimension, some will use the new frequencies for new skills not available in the third dimension. For those who cannot adjust to the higher dimension, their ascension experience will be different.

"Do the new frequencies cause what is known as 'ascension symptoms'?" I asked.

"Yes, in a way, they do," Cerian said. "The ascension symptoms are unique to bodies adjusting to different frequencies. There is much hype about what they are and aren't, and there is confusion around that."

People adjusting to the different energies may experience sensations that some refer to as ascension symptoms. These may be physical (e.g., vertigo, rashes, joint pain), emotional (e.g., anxiety attacks), mental (e.g., sadness, irritability), or even psychic/spiritual (e.g., seeing extraterrestrials or spirits, communicating with animals).

Do not label a symptom as a disease or attach yourself to a disease state (e.g., say, "I am feeling joint pain," rather than "I have arthritic pain") because by doing so, you may manifest arthritis, but be gentle with yourself if you do label "it." The sensations will vary from person to person and can be minor to extreme.

The way I approach ascension symptoms is that if I experience any indication that I may be sick, I seek medical advice to rule out a health challenge. Once I've exercised reasonable exploration and have not found a medical condition, I consider that I may be experiencing an ascension symptom. I asked Cerian if this approach was a fair way of dealing with this.

They (Cerian) responded, "Yes."

You may also have increased levels of "Light" coming into your body. Light is the energy of Source or God's Energy and permeates all levels of consciousness. Your sleep patterns may likely disrupt, increasing fatigue. As always, take care of yourself. Listen to your body, for it knows what you need.

DOES DIET IMPACT MY ASCENSION?

Many communicating about the New Earth suggest that one must refrain from eating meats, sugar, and consuming alcohol. What we ingest does impact our blood and cells. One does not need to be a food scientist to know that the cleaner we eat, the cleaner our energies.

In any case, Daniel said, "It is not critical. One may continue to vibrate, but perhaps not as fast, or it may take a little longer." In other words, diet does impact your energy, but it may simply take longer for a person who consumes unclean foodstuff to evolve.

Early in my life, I adopted the attitude of everything in moderation and nothing in extreme. I've never practiced diets, and I consume meat from time to time, although I have cut back. I also enjoy a glass of Cabernet Sauvignon and dark chocolate. I do make every effort to have the right relationship with anything I consume, meaning I bless my food.

What's most important is that everyone's experience will be unique. We should listen to our bodies. They will tell us what is appropriate for us to consume. What we eat and drink is a personal decision, and others should not drive our choices; after all, we are all sovereign beings.

CHAPTER 7:

Accessing the New Earth

You manifest every day, for you are a creator
Believe that the New Earth is here, and
within you is the key to accessing it.
—Connie

"HOW CAN ONE ACCESS the New Earth?" I asked Daniel in a channeling.

"You can access the New Earth by changing your perspective. Be open to the possibility that something new is coming in."

Adopt the belief that anything can happen. Throw out limiting views that things have to make sense because the simple truth is that New Earth experiences are beyond our current affairs and won't make sense.

I've had my fair share of odd situations in my life and, at first, wondered if I had lost my mind. I've had items disappear in my household only to reappear in the same place days later. I've had things move from one room to another, mysterious lit candles, improbable synchronicities, even books showing up in my house with no explanation of how they got there, yet when read, the books gave me profound messages.

Those times when strange things have happened to you or around you, and you sought to explain them with logic, are likely times you've flirted with the fourth or fifth dimension. So please stop trying to diminish the miracles and consider the possibility that something miraculous is occurring. I like to *expect the unexpected*.

Albert Einstein once said, "There are only two ways to live your life. One is as though *nothing* is a miracle. The other is as though *everything* is a miracle." Have you tried to take the latter approach? I guarantee you if you do, your world will shift, and these little miracles will multiply. The New Earth is here for us to experience. As an observer, watch for and expect the miracles.

LAW OF ATTRACTION

The Law of Attraction, part of the New Thought philosophy from the early nineteenth century, gained great exposure with the film and book's release of *The Secret* in 2006. The heart of the philosophy is "like attracts like energy," based on the belief that positive thoughts bring positive experiences while negative thinking brings negative experiences.

Yet, we know belief is energy. All energy has a particular frequency, which is a component of the Law of Vibration. Believing goes beyond keeping our thoughts positive and "fake it till you make it," the act of emulating competence, confidence, and an optimistic mindset that a person can achieve the qualities they seek in their life. Believing something with our "heart and soul" carries a more substantial causative effect, assuring it will happen.

Keeping thoughts positive and being optimistic does shift the frequency. Keep your thoughts positive and *believe* that the New Earth is here and you have access to it.

Daniel continued sharing about accessing the New Earth, "Be aware of your emotions and feelings you are experiencing to identify whether they are releasing those with fear or with love and sovereignty."

Everything is energy, including emotions and feelings, and as noted, energy vibrates at a frequency. When experiencing feelings of fear that vibrate at about 100 Hz, we lower our frequency, whereas love vibrates at 500 Hz. The frequency of the New Earth is higher than our third dimension. Fear will keep you in the third dimension. In contrast, claiming your sovereignty and feeling love, compassion, peace, and joy will raise your vibration and increase your awareness of the higher dimensions and the miracles around you.

You are a sovereign being. You have supreme power over your body, mind, and spirit. Claim your sovereignty. We'll chat more about this in the chapters to come.

THE POWER OF BELIEF
BY CONNIE

We can manifest our reality if we believe. I heard this several times, and I never truly understood or believed this until I experienced it.

Several years ago, a coworker shared her thoughts about the Law of Attraction and manifestation. She felt it was a bunch of hogwash because nothing ever seemed to go her way. As I sat back silently agreeing with her, energy began vibrating and buzzing in my head. I wasn't sure what it was, but I sat straight up and focused.

"Are you okay?" my coworker asked.

All of a sudden, to my surprise, words started flowing from my mouth. "You don't think that you can create or manifest because you have too many rules, expectations, and judgments. Think of it this way: what you want is in the astral realms, and you need to bring it down here to 3D to access it.

"Let's do an exercise, shall we?" I continued. "I'd like for you to imagine that there are *three ice cream cones* in the astral realm. Think about how much you want those ice cream cones. Don't think about how much they cost, how you will get them, or the calories. Just think about how much you want them and how happy you'll be when you taste them. One of the biggest keys to manifestation is belief and imagination. Unfortunately, we are taught in school that imagination is nonsense or child's play."

I sat there confused, wondering where that information came from and how it just flowed through me. "Take what resonates," I mumbled.

The following day, my coworker approached and shared her magical evening.

"I did the ice cream experiment!" she said excitedly. "About an hour after I set my intention, my husband comes home with a package of ice cream cones. Get this—it was a package of four; my husband's client took one cone and gave him the *three* remaining ice cream cones.

"But that isn't the best part!" she continued. "As I finished my ice cream, I repeated the exercise, imagining that I'd receive $2,287.15 to repay us on an uncollectible loan."

For several years, my coworker and her husband had been unsuccessful in collecting the money owed to them.

"Would you believe that a few hours after eating my ice cream, there was a knock at our door? It was the debtor who was very apologetic and gave us a check for $2,287.16.

My coworker had no idea how the debtor even found them because they had moved. I find it quite funny how, in this manifestation, she received an extra penny in the repayment, almost as if the Universe was saying, "Keep the change!"

I went home that evening and wondered what had happened. "Is that all it takes to manifest? It can't be! It sounds too easy."

I brought a keyboard to my son, Daniel.

He typed, "Ice cream lesson not just for your coworker, but for your doubting mind as well." Daniel added that we manifest even when we are unaware we are doing it.

When I pressed Daniel for more details, he typed, "Pull out your diary and look through what you wrote in February 1999."

I had forgotten about my diary and retrieved it from the safe; a bit tickled that my son knew about it. I read through February. It had been a difficult period for me. I lived with someone who had fallen out of love with me. We were going through a breakup. I was in a new city with no money and my severely autistic son. I wrote in my diary that I needed $4,000 to get a place for a fresh start.

I continued reading the journal entries into the following month and was floored when I read this:

"Dear Diary,

I can't believe what happened. I was sitting on the couch crying and wondering how Daniel and I were going to make it. All of a sudden, the phone rings. It is the Social Security office. I thought they were calling because it was time to renew the case. However, the lady on the phone said that she was doing an audit and noticed that there had been an enormous error on Daniel's case and that he was due $4,100 in back pay. The deposit will be in the account in less than two weeks. I'm so happy."

For me, the moral of the story is that we are *creators and manifesters,* and it took some yummy ice cream, years after the fact, to see it. I wouldn't have even noticed it if my son hadn't told me where to look in my diary.

I know this is the case for everyone. We manifest things every day yet don't realize it. Consider this. Be aware. You are a creator. Can you believe that the New Earth is here, and *within you* is the key to accessing it?

CHAPTER 8:

The New Earth Experience

You may want to save everyone and preach about the New Earth. The best thing you can do is live authentically and permit others to do the same.

I ASKED DANIEL a series of questions about how people will experience the New Earth and how they'll experience those who don't encounter it, and vice versa. For simplification, I use "left behind" to clarify those remaining in third-dimensional consciousness. I use "ascending" for those experiencing the New Earth consciousness.

HOW WILL THOSE ASCENDING
EXPERIENCE THOSE LEFT BEHIND?

"Daniel, for those people going to the New Earth, those ascending, how will they experience people who don't go?"

Daniel shared, "They may not experience them. In other words, they may not be in their life any longer, whether it be family or a friend. For whatever reason, they may drift apart or be in communication infrequently with each other. It will be a gradual separation, and it will not be painful. It will just be that there is nothing in common."

This information contradicts what some have communicated about those left behind. Others speculate that a separation will form two Earths, where one ends in ascension and the other in cataclysmic destruction. According to Daniel, this is not the case.

Considering that everything is probability and possibility, there will not be that extreme separation of heaven and destruction in my timeline and reality. That does not mean that life for those not ascending will be peaches and cream. It could mean that life becomes more challenging and complex.

Perhaps you have seen friends or family slowly disappearing from your life. Your interests no longer are the same. Your engagement with them is diminishing. Maybe your views are considered too radical, or you are too "woo-woo." (I can relate to this term.)

You, your friends, and your family have unique blueprints. You may be here to experience the New Earth while they may not be. Respect their choices. Each needs to stand in their Truth and live their blueprint. There is no judgment if a friend or family member chooses to remain on the third-dimensional Earth. It is not a bad thing. It is a choice.

HOW WILL THOSE PEOPLE LEFT BEHIND EXPERIENCE THOSE ASCENDING?

"Daniel, how about those *not going* to the New Earth?" I began. "How will they experience those choosing to go?"

Daniel shared, "The term 'go' is loaded. They are not going anywhere. They are already here but will perceive that their life continues as it always has, that they will have the trials and tribulations and have their same thoughts and feelings, and it will be as it has always been. There will not be that huge shift."

In the hours upon hours of channelings, the message that the New Earth is here has been consistent. We aren't going anywhere. We are here, yet we need to change our perspective to experience the New Earth.

Daniel continued, "They may perceive those who are stepping into the new world as 'way out there' or moving in a different cycle, a more prosperous cycle. There may be some judgmental resentment from that, but then again, both parties will be drifting from each other, as there is no longer the cord connecting them. Whether familial, friend, or work, there will be a gradual shift."

I am aware that my views, particularly over the last twenty-five years, have become what many people view as woo-woo.

I think it is a criterion for changing one's perspective. To have an awareness of the higher dimensions, one needs to be open to all possibilities.

The message was constant that there will be a separation between those stepping into the higher frequencies of love, peace, and enlightenment (ascending), and those choosing the lower frequencies, which keep people in fear, control, and darkness (left behind).

WILL THOSE PEOPLE LEFT BEHIND RETURN TO EARTH AFTER THEY'VE TRANSITIONED?

"Daniel, will those not ascending to the higher dimensions return to Earth after they've passed away?" I asked.

"It is up to every one of them," Daniel says. "It is how the individual reflects upon their experiences here on Earth and whether they have fulfilled what they came here to learn."

"So, they won't go to a different planet?" I asked.

"They may or they may not, depending again if they have lived true to what they came here to experience."

The theme that each person has their unique blueprint was consistent. We engaged in compelling dialogues about people being on different paths and having infinite purposes. Our humanity wants to save everyone and educate about the "right" choice so that our loved ones experience the New Heavens and New Earth. However, there isn't a right choice. The closest thing to right is living authentically to the purpose or divine blueprint we have come here to fulfill. A person's blueprint may very well be to experience life in the 3D physical for their growth.

We cannot judge where people are in this shift.

MY PARTNER AND I ARE ON DIFFERENT PATHS. SHOULD WE SEPARATE?

I often hear that people are concerned that their loved ones are on different paths. They want their partners to understand what they believe about the ascension. Some want to save them. Alternatively, others smother their beliefs, find a middle ground because their thoughts and desires impact their relationships. They don't want to risk losing their significant others. These feelings aren't limited to partners and can extend to other family members, children, parents, siblings, friends, and coworkers.

If individuals come into this life and it is in their blueprint to experience the shift in consciousness, they may have loved ones on a different life path. There are many different blueprints, and the loved one's role may be to witness the shift in consciousness, not to experience it, and remain in the 3D through this shift. There is no judgment in this situation, as this may be why they are here.

According to Daniel, if one is on a path of ascension, meaning it is in their blueprint to experience the shift, and they are with someone who is not on that path, then "they must move apart and do other things." At risk is the work they came here to do to be sovereign. Remaining with one on a different path may change their desire to experience the shift and, consequently, not fully experience who and what they are. They may miss the mark and not fulfill their spiritual blueprint.

Ask yourself, "Am I on an ascension path?" If you have been drawn to this book, you likely are.

During this ascension, people may become separated from loved ones. This parting is not something that would occur overnight. It could be over their lifetime. It is also dependent on how willing a person is to embrace the work they need to do to raise their energetic frequency to become sovereign. It is also a choice.

CHAPTER 9:

Tips and Next Steps for Ascension

Do not go outward to seek guidance from others. Always listen to the voice within.
—Daniel

LIVE YOUR TRUTH

THE MOST SIGNIFICANT thing anyone can do to assist on their ascension journey is to live their Truth. What I mean by this is to live your most authentic self. Do things daily that bring you joy. You are worth it! When doing this, you become a beneficial presence to the world because you become a walking expression of your soul's calling. What do I mean? Follow your heart.

Energetically, to live your Truth means that you merge with the higher heart chakra, which may be known to you as the etheric heart or the seat of the soul. The higher heart chakra is at the thymus gland, which sits between the heart and the sternum. It is here that we can discern *our* Truth.

If you are unclear about your Truth or blueprint, know that the higher heart can lead you to it vibrationally. It is the most accurate compass to your soul's calling. Most have inklings of their blueprint, but trust your intuition, that inner knowing from the soul and Source, if you aren't sure.

To put it differently, Daniel shared, "A person is closer to their actual genetic blueprint when harmonized with the frequencies that resonate with them."

It has taken me years to understand this. In my earlier years, I would have asked a psychic, "What's my purpose in life?" Today I know that my inner guidance is more accurate than any psychic's guidance on this matter. Everyone has the same mission, and that is to live *their* blueprint. Don't ask a psychic. You are the only one who can determine this. The answers are within, and everyone can discern this using their intuition, psychic senses, or reflecting on what brings one joy.

Some find answers when asking for guidance with their psychic senses, like clairaudience (inner voices and thoughts), clairvoyance (visions), clairsentience (gut feelings and hunches), and so on. Keep in mind that psychic hits process through your filters. The information is highly accurate if your filters are clean, free of biases, prejudices, false beliefs, and ego.

Alternatively, your intuition, or knowing without conscious reasoning, is from your higher self, and we often overlook it. Unlike psychic hits, intuition is guidance from the soul. Trust it. Pay attention to it. Let your soul lead the way, and you will quickly learn.

Cerian shares, "It is by your very nature of standing in your Truth that you are in resonance with your harmonic chord. When more and more people resonate by living their Truth, individually, they are a note. Collectively, they are a symphony. They are a harmony. They put out a new frequency, a vibrational pattern within the Earth."

Living our Truth aligns our frequency, and we become part of something much bigger than we can imagine. We not only assist in our ascension, but we become beacons for those around us. Each of us, when awakened, plays an individual note. Collectively we create a symphony, a new frequency or vibrational pattern that will awaken others and set a course to reach that critical number needed to reveal the beauty, magnificence, and awe of the New Earth.

Cerian urged that it is vital to be in resonance with your blueprint of why you are here. Everyone has a unique note. Everyone is needed.

"However you perceive that Truth, whether through thought, sound, physical experience, or projecting, listen and go within. Do *not* go outward to seek guidance from others. Always go in and listen to the voice that sits within you. That is what you can do right here and now."

Daniel urged through facilitated communication:

"Acknowledge the Truth of others.
We must see the Truth of others and
allow them to have their consciousness, their process, their experience, whomever they may be. You have
no idea what their Truth is. That
will allow you to have an even deeper
connection within yourself when you
let go of others outside of you."

Daniel's message may seem complex, but it is quite simple yet challenging for us as humans. We are not here to judge others. We are here to follow our hearts and play our roles, not condemn the actions of others (or ourselves). We cannot understand the scope of the events unfolding on this planet. Everything is connected. As the systems, those organized frameworks we follow, fall apart and rebuild, we need to stay in our own lane.

There will always be the hero, villain, and victim in any good tale, along with a host of other roles. This setup is valid for this game of life to reveal the New Earth. No one role is any more important than another. You must play your part well while not judging the actions of others.

Events are in place to shift humanity to new heights. These events will likely bring situations that create fear and angst for many. Be the hero who stands in calmness, peace, and love amid chaos. While in turmoil, be an observer, not a participant. Be compassionate for others that stand opposite of you.

Always honor your Truth. Speak and stand in your Truth. Do so in a way that honors other people's Truth in compassion, empathy, and love.

MAKING PEACE WITH THINGS
THAT CAUSE SUFFERING

Daniel stated, "Make peace with the way all entities are programmed," which can be challenging to understand, particularly when something has caused great suffering. I asked Daniel in a subsequent channeling what tips he could share to help us be peaceful with things that bring great anguish and hardship. This is what he shared.

"The tip would be: Do not stand in fear, for fear is the biggest sin. Remember that everything is light, frequency, and energy. Do not judge whatever has shaken you up. Understand and repeat that you are whole and have everything you need, and *there is nothing for you to lose*. This is all an illusion, and you *are* a creator and can manifest that which you need.

"The problem with most people is that they *assume* they need much more because they are outward-facing rather than inward-facing. They focus on what's outside of them rather than what's inside. And so, it becomes a necessity to play in this world that is an illusion. They get caught up in it and jump into fear because they are not playing in their role of being a creator."

Daniel's tips are to:

1. Stand in your Truth.
2. Take time to go inward through meditation, breathing, and mindfulness.
3. Honor your intuition, your higher self.
4. Do not judge.
5. Recognize that everything is energy.
6. Realize that the illusion is that *we* bought into creating these systems that now need to come apart to express our evolved growth.
7. Do not be afraid of change.

CHAPTER 10:

Subtle Indications You Are Shifting to 5D

When embodying your true self, your frequency shifts and you live authentically, joyfully, shining your light.

AS MENTIONED EARLIER, many expect the shift to the New Earth, or the fifth dimension, to be a significant noticeable change, like ascending to an entirely different world where one will live in bliss without challenges. That is not quite the case. For most, the process of shifting isn't likened to one giant step but relatively tiny movements forward, with occasional adjustments back before continuing one's evolution. Moving or shifting into higher dimensions means you are operating on a new frequency, yet your frequency fluctuates.

Some of the signs indicating you are shifting are subtle, while others aren't. The following are some of the ways subtle shifts can happen.

THROUGH LESSONS AND RESOLVING TRAUMAS, PEACE EMERGES.

Our challenges or our soul's lessons can help trigger us to move to higher states of consciousness. As you identify traumas or denser energies related to your lessons and work them out, your frequency changes, and you become lighter. When these disturbances emerge in your life, they indicate you are ready to shift a level, and the lessons are your springboard.

Once you begin healing your traumas and subconscious beliefs, you'll likely glimpse the true meaning of inner peace. And that will become the new gold standard and priority in your life. You may seek ways to keep your energy balanced by deepening your meditation practice, spending time in nature, exercising, practicing mindfulness, or making changes in your life to provide situations that permit you to continue this inner peace.

As the traumas resolve, you will experience energy cleansings as your physical self has exchanges with the higher self, the soul. You can step into your inner power by cleaning out the energy that isn't serving. Your thoughts are clearer, and you may even feel lighter because you've elevated your frequency.

YOU BECOME MORE SENSITIVE TO ENERGY.

As you shift, you'll notice that you're more sensitive to energy, and you'll prefer being in higher vibrational energy (though you may not know it). You'll find you may choose to be in certain places while disliking being in other areas for no particular reason. You may feel depleted being around certain people or places and find more fulfillment being alone more often, strengthening your vibration. You essentially become more clairsentient.

When learning that everything is energy, including yourself, at some point, you'll devote yourself to strengthening your power. You'll become more aware that certain situations, environments, work, and even people may negatively impact your energy. Given that it is now a priority to maintain that inner peace, you'll want to make changes to strengthen your energetic body, resulting in changes in relationships, work, or even your living environment.

Another indication that you are flirting with higher realms is when you find yourself observing rather than participating in circumstances in your life. By stepping aside and allowing some distance between you and your situation, you permit a higher awareness to guide you, and better alternatives emerge rather than those knee-jerk reactions.

YOUR FRIENDSHIPS AND RELATIONSHIPS CHANGE.

As your energetic frequency changes, you will notice people coming in and out of your life. On the one hand, you will find yourself not engaging with some people you have known for years, even family. There is a bit of a disconnect from them. While on the other hand, you will also find that, like a breath of fresh air, new people will emerge in your life, and you may even recognize a soul connection with them. You'll feel comfortable genuinely expressing who you are to them and become empowered by expressing your true self.

It is only natural to want to save your family and friends, so they experience the shift to the fifth dimension. Unfortunately, you cannot. It is not in everyone's blueprint to shift. Some are here to witness the change, while others have different roles. Each chooses their experience. It is essential to respect their decisions and free will. If you share some of your beliefs and experiences with someone you care about and they are genuinely interested in learning more, your help is encouraged. On the other hand, your support is not welcome if the exchange energetically depletes you or if they are hesitant or resistant to the information. It is not your job to save everyone.

At some point, you will realize that you choose lessons at the soul level. Many of these lessons involve loved ones. This realization is a leap in your spiritual journey. Rather than worrying about loved ones and praying for a specific outcome for their situation, send them love, and if praying, pray for the highest and best development for their soul's journey.

HONOR YOUR INTUITION AND FOLLOW YOUR HEART.
As you elevate your frequency and flirt with the higher dimensions, your intuition, that inner knowing from your

higher self, strengthens. It will become easier to recognize your Truth and discern your blueprint by following your heart. You may even feel a quickening at times, a warmth or vibration in your heart, communicating with you or showing the way. By honoring both that inner knowing and your heart, your path becomes divinely guided and illumined.

You will realize at some point that you have been hiding, likely because you haven't felt safe to live authentically. Quenching your true essence, of course, hampers you in many situations: your career, relationships, finances, or simply by leaving your energy open to energy vampires that steal your energy. When not living authentically, you *do not* live your blueprint or tap into your inner power to benefit your life. A sign that you're shifting is when you say, "enough is enough," and realize you are powerful enough to overcome the insecurities of living your true self. You leap and follow your heart.

Once doing so, you likely will feel that you are here to help others. You realize, though, that preaching your Truth isn't the way. You are here to "be," to demonstrate your true self, which is how you help others. As you embody more and more of your true spirit, your soul's energy, your frequency changes, you live authentically and are joyful, which indicates you are shining your light and walking your talk.

CHAPTER 11:

Strengthen Your 5D Experience

*Experience life in a way that you don't
seek anything. Be present and let things
evolve naturally without forcing it.*

WE TRAVEL IN AND OUT of dimensions. Some are on a
path of ascension or here to experience the New Earth. The
New Earth is ready, but most of us haven't fully arrived. We
may ascend the dimensions from the third, fourth, to the fifth
but fall back down to the third dimension because we haven't
stabilized in 5D.

I asked Daniel in channeling what we could do to extend
our time in the fifth dimension. Some of this material I

mentioned in earlier chapters, but I wanted to summarize his suggestions here. The biggest tip he gave was to experience life. However, to do it in a way that you don't seek anything, be present and let things evolve naturally without forcing it.

Here are some suggestions to help move you into the fifth dimension and keep you there more and more.

Be aware – Be available to know what is happening around you in your life. Learn safely through observation, awareness, and mindfulness. Our awareness is a catalyst to change and transform. Without awareness, we remain in the status quo. With awareness, we empower ourselves to evolve.

Be present – There is only the now. Refrain from pondering events in your past or future. Eternity (timelessness) is in the moment and gained when appreciating with deep gratitude what you have *now*.

Be non-judging – We are not here to judge the actions of others or ourselves. We are here to follow our hearts and live our Truth. Combatting judgment is part of this spiritual journey, and the tools are compassion, empathy, love, and kindness.

Be curious – Ask questions, and be curious about everything because the answers will take you places you haven't gone before. It will also help you understand emotions better. Curiosity awakens you to know yourself and your genuine relationship with Source. There is much power in asking questions.

Be open – Being open is seeing things as they are and how they *could* make your life exciting. The truth is fluid. It changes as we grow. If we are so stubborn to refuse to consider things, we will not evolve. One cannot open their heart unless one is willing to consider new ideas.

Be playful – Exercise childlike enthusiasm, awe, and wonder when observing your world. By being playful, the burdens within diminish, and you open your mind and heart. When watching with awe and expectation, you see the magic, mystery, and miracles in everything, and life becomes joyful. You are here to experience. Why not enjoy it?

PART III

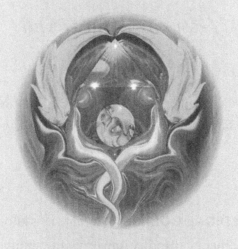

Autism

CHAPTER 12:

Pure Autism

*The Autists bring New Earth energy and New
Planetary consciousness, and both need anchoring.*
—Daniel

IN THE MEDICAL COMMUNITY, autism is known as a serious developmental disorder impairing the ability to communicate and interact. I am here to tell you that this definition is wrong. It is not a disorder. It is not a disease. Pure Autism is a species in itself. I'm sure I lost just about everyone, but please bear with me here.

This information came through Shauna Kalicki while channeling Daniel. As you will see, Daniel verified its accuracy and provided more details through facilitated communication.

There is such a thing as Pure Autism, and those with it I refer to as the Pure Autists. Since humankind came to this planet, the Pure Autists have been on Earth, first in thought in Lemuria, then form. They are a species by themselves. They are here for a reason, and this section of the book involves their work for our ascension and the New Earth.

For a human, when the soul's spark of life enters the human form, from the very moment of conception and until the ages of four and five, and maybe as old as seven, the soul *lightly* attaches to the physicality. Then, that spark of life embeds and identifies with its physical form, but until then, it *lightly* connects.

The Pure Autists, however, never fully engrain in their physicality. They always will remain disconnected from their form at varying degrees. This disconnect permits them to experience life significantly differently from humans entrenched in their bodies.

Daniel shares, "The Pure Autist calibration of their energy and mind into physicality is like putting a jet engine on a go-cart." The body can't handle the Pure Autist energy, so they are tethered to their bodies but not deeply in them.

The Pure Autist can be lightly attached to their physicality, empowering them to experience life in a landscape that humans can't fathom. Their reality includes seeing time and space, other dimensions, planets, other universes, and communing with other Autists, angels, Masters, galactic beings, and aliens. They are indeed a species on their own and in no way diseased or "less than" humans.

Throughout humankind's history, the Pure Autists have come to grid the planet and work with the energies. They've also worked on projects in ancient Mayan, Peruvian, and some Native American cultures, even the indigenous Aborigines. The fascinating thing about the assistance of the Pure Autists during these ancient projects is that they were energies coming into the world and not attached to a single form or body. They were pure consciousness. They had no bodies.

In Lemuria, as the energies began to shift, new harmonic energies, vibrations, patterns, and sacred geometries came in, and there was a need for more Pure Autists to come who were less in their bodies. During the Lemurian and Atlantean times, some achieved great things during periods of shifting and transitioning because they were not so attached to their physicality and were not so "brain-centered."

Cerian added that the Autists were part of the creation of many sacred sites around the world. They were also energetically connected to creating a mystical school in Lemuria that continued through many generations. These Pure Autists were more in their auric field, in consciousness, and that is where the Pure Autists stayed. (The auric field consists of multiple layers of consciousness extending beyond a physical body.)

There has been and still is a call for the Autists to come in. Although they have been here throughout time, the Pure Autists have not been understood. Instead of seeing them as a different species engaged in other dimensions, people only saw that they were not in control of their bodies, perceived as incapable of intelligent reasoning. They were labeled simple-minded, stupid, uncoordinated, schizophrenic, retarded, diseased, autistic, and more. They were institutionalized, "living" their lives in the corner of a room.

The truth is that Pure Autists are energetic beings who are different from humans. The Autist's body cannot handle all the Pure Autist energies coming into them, which is one of the reasons they remain in the higher realms. If they did fully embody their energies, they could, in a way, fry out their circuits. Like humans, Pure Autists are also evolving, and while it has taken some time, some Autists today can better integrate their Pure Autist energy with their bodies.

Much of the Autist energy coming to Earth today is an energetic vibrational pattern that has waited for more evolved amped-up bodies to handle Pure Autist energy. Many Pure Autists are currently coming to the planet because it is different energy needed for humanity's ascension. Humankind will also benefit from the Pure Autists' abilities to see between the dimensions and time and space.

When asking Daniel about this part of the channeled information, he not only graded it as accurate, he typed the following:

"The Pure Autist energy needs to be anchored. The Earth itself is only ascending. The Earth has one consciousness, it is one being, one intelligence, and because of its vastness, it takes humanity with it, elevating all of humanity. The Autists and Gaia work in tandem. We (Pure Autists) are part of the New Earth Consciousness discussed for many years now. The Autists not only bring New Earth energy but New Planetary consciousness, and both need anchoring.

"Very few Autists originate from Earth. Most are from other places. We, Autists, are bringing down this planetary consciousness. Other humans don't do this as their memory is wiped from the motherboard. That doesn't happen with the Autists, especially the new ones coming down. This will get stronger and stronger and has not happened before. This is epic!"

For clarification, throughout this book, the word "Autist(s)" (uppercase "A") denotes an individual(s) with Pure Autism. Most Autists are not from Earth and are starseeds, which is explained in the next chapter.

CHAPTER 13:

Pure Autism vs. Medically-Induced Autism

*No matter what, autism was supposed
to happen. There are no accidents.*
—Daniel

PURE AUTISM IS NOT A DISORDER or disease and is meant
to be here. Pure Autists are not accidents. It is a divine gift to
humanity that has not been understood. Historically, humankind fears what we don't understand. So to appease that fear,
we created a story that we could comprehend, and that story
is that autism is a disorder. It isn't.

Pure Autism was part of the plan for the game of life. Many writers advocate that childhood vaccinations cause autism. There is some truth to this, but much of it is not understood. It is part of the planetary shift in consciousness, and childhood vaccinations can *trigger* a child's DNA or genetic makeup to manifest Pure Autism. However, the simple truth is that if a child's destiny is to be a Pure Autist, their autism will manifest, whether immunized or not. Childhood immunizations, however, can also injure innocent children.

CHILDHOOD VACCINATIONS

Most vaccinations start with good intentions and have saved countless lives. However, the unfortunate downside of *any* immunization is the potential side effects.

The complicated part is that while the immunizations can trigger Pure Autism, they can also trigger *side effects* in some children that *mimic* the characteristics of Pure Autists. Consequently, many children manifesting the Pure Autists' *characteristics* were diagnosed with autism, but they are not Pure Autists.

I call those harmed by the immunizations medically-induced autistics. These children (many now adults) are genuinely disabled. They have had their neural networks scrambled and genetic DNA structures changed. For those autistics whose neural network was manipulated through vaccinations, their cells and brain impacted their blood, triggering changes in their DNA.

The medically-induced autistics contribute to the unprecedented increase in autism, going from one in five thousand (1980) to 1 in fifty-four (2016). This phenomenon is *partly* responsible for the rise in the autism rate. The other side to this is that more Pure Autists are needed, more than ever, to do their work for the planetary ascension. And Daniel says that more Pure Autists are coming in.

So, the question becomes, where do you want to hang your hat? Do you want to believe the vaccination's side effects were unintentional? Or do you want to consider there is a dark side and light side of humanity wanting to manipulate humans as part of a spiritual war, to stop the ascension so that some can continue their control of humankind?

There is no right or wrong way to look at this. Whether you choose to believe it was unintentional or dark and devious, understand that there is a significant opportunity for growth here. Forgive and be compassionate for those involved with the vaccinations. Send unconditional love to the victims, the families, and the perpetrators. Remember, this is an illusion, and consider that it is all a part of the plan for planetary evolution.

Regarding this topic, Daniel typed, "No matter what, this was supposed to happen. There are no accidents."

Please keep in mind that you are a sovereign being, and vaccinations are a personal choice. The individual (or parent), not any government or institution, should decide whether to get vaccinations. On one level, vaccinations have saved countless lives. On another level, they have caused changes to individuals' bodies, resulting in devastating results for the children and their families. Some people can absorb the ingredients injected in a vaccination, while others cannot, leading to illnesses, allergies, and chronic conditions.

As humanity begins to shift energetically, the Pure Autists hope that humans will not need vaccinations and can automatically attune their energies to burn up or stop viruses, germs, and bacteria.

CHAPTER 14:

Autists and the New Earth

No matter how limited or disabled the Autist body is, our minds are completely free. Most of the time, we Autists are aware of our capacity to be free.
—Daniel

ENTER THE I AM

THERE WAS ONE CHANNELING SESSION that was a bit unusual. The information came in from a voice claiming to be "I AM." This was a first, and it explained that I AM included Cerian and Daniel and acknowledged that the names of the various entities ("energy streams") that Shauna had channeled over time were for her benefit.

When I think about it, it makes sense. As humans, we want to label everything, but the simple truth is that everything goes back to Source, God, the I AM, including you, because we are all One.

"Many Autists work with energies and frequencies and align to them easily because it is without form." The I AM continued, "This is especially true for the Autists you work with, though there are many other groups."

The Ethereal Autists are creating with the energies. While they may work with the higher realms' energies, the "dramatic change" we seek, the shift to the New Earth, must occur in the physical form.

Many Autists on the planet currently do not identify with their physical form because of its density. The Ethereal Autist is not wholly in its physical form and resides in the higher dimensions. They have not fully embodied. They "must lower their ability to work with these energies." Yet, they cannot quickly rise out into the higher realms if they are in physical form. Therefore, they remain *lightly* in physicality.

Of course, if an Autist is not tied strongly to their physicality, their caregivers will likely witness problems associated with their bodies. For example, at one time, Daniel almost ran into heavy traffic, causing Connie to invest in a Posey belt that would offer more security to keep him safe.

We can't imagine what these Ethereal Autists are engaged in, and it makes the caregiver's job challenging to keep them safe.

French philosopher Pierre Teilhard de Chardin said, "We are not human beings having a spiritual experience; we are spiritual beings having a human experience." Consider for a moment that *you* are *a spiritual being having a physical experience.* You created and manifested your world, but it is an illusion. Your perceived illusion is a slowing down of an energy source so that you have slow motion, solidity, firmness, and density. You are physical and can't imagine being in the etheric, spiritual, or energetic realm. Still, that realm is where the Ethereal Autists reside, and just as we have difficulty experiencing that energetic realm, the Ethereal Autist is challenged to experience physicality.

Not all Autists (of Pure Autism) have aligned themselves in such a way to permit separation from their body into the ethereal realm. In other words, some Autists remain in the physical, while others work within the energetic field and manipulate energies so that the energies accelerate.

Ethereal Autists are unique in that they work with colors and energies. Some of humanity is aware of these energies and moves in and out of them, but not most people. The Ethereal Autists understand that pure creation depends on vibrational light, color, and speed. They also can identify what is needed now on Earth in this shift in consciousness. They plot and observe, and Pure Autism is another expressional form of beingness.

New energies are coming to Earth, and the Ethereal Autists understand these energies far better than those heavily entrenched in the third dimension. They work with the energies so that they resonate with other energies. Mother Mary shared that the Ethereal Autists weave energy and frequencies. The new "energies coming in are being worked with so that humanity as a whole can survive, use them, tap into them, can also work with them."

The Ethereal Autists understand the energy's intent and purpose because it is pure consciousness. As the Ethereal Autists weave the energy, a spectrum of colors, vibrations, and frequencies emerge. Some people may even experience this color intensification. The Ethereal Autists use this energy to create a harmonic so that humanity can use the new energies to help with their awakening. Without the Autists' influence on energy, humankind would not wake up in time, and humanity's consciousness would fall, losing any opportunity for ascension.

The awakened Autists working in the ethers, or Ethereal Autists, are a unique species. They are a bridge that allows humankind to use the new energy coming to the planet to awaken humanity.

According to Mother Mary, to experience the New Earth, our perception while in physical form must change because the "dramatic change" must occur while in physicality. The New Earth is in an etheric state. Humanity also resides within an etheric state—only it does not acknowledge it. It is up to us to expand our perceptions, sense that the New Earth is here, and resonate with it.

A person who experiences the shift will impact those around them. As the change occurs within one person, the patterning of the New Earth's etheric levels and the physicality blending push out more energy for others. The spiritual merges with the physical.

It is vital to expand your awareness, knowing the New Earth is here and the changes are already happening. Don't expect something from the outside to occur. In other words, don't expect a savior to emerge and bring humanity to the New Earth. It already is happening from within each of us. And it is up to each of us to claim our sovereignty and choose the New Earth experience.

A NEW SPECTRUM

This book is not about the autistic as an individual with a developmental disorder or disability. According to the psychiatric community, autism spectrum disorder (ASD) is a complex developmental condition involving continuous communication, social interaction, and behavioral challenges. The effects of ASD and the severity of symptoms are different in each person.

Mother Mary does describe a spectrum, though it is a bit different from mental health professionals. According to Mother Mary, some autistics come into this world less embodied. These are what society refers to as low functioning. Many of these are "awakened" Autists who work with the energies, as Daniel does. They are the Ethereal Autists.

Simultaneously, other autistics have come into this life a little more embodied than those on the high end of the spectrum. That group of Autists serves in the consciousness shift as a bridge between the higher realms (the Ethereal Autists) and humanity. One can think of them as Bridge Autists.

Then there are other autistics whom society labels Asperger's. These individuals are on the low end of the spectrum and considered high functioning. They understand how to participate in this "reality." They control their bodies, yet they are still not fully integrated. These high-functioning Autists work with specific energies that are creative catalysts to shift consciousness. Some of them are aware that they are doing this work. Others are not aware, but, in both cases, they assist humanity in ways society does not understand. One can think of this group as Catalytic Autists, not Asperger's, because it is not a neurodevelopmental disorder.

Within the spectrum of Autists, there is a larger plan that involves raising the consciousness of humanity. That is not the subject for this book, though perhaps, I will explore it in others. Right now, consider that Pure Autists on all parts of the spectrum—the Ethereal, Bridge, and Catalytic Autists—either knowingly or unknowingly work in the shift of the planet's consciousness.

Many Autists work with humanity, but not all people. Some people are aware of and want this shift in consciousness and are asking for it, while others do not want to see it. It is free will. Those choosing to remain in the third dimension may remain aloof, independent, and separate, believing they are in control. They are, in essence, in control of themselves, but they do influence others.

Daniel said, "One must always be aware of free will. Many choose the assistance of the Awesome Ones (what Daniel calls the Pure Autists), and many don't choose the assistance of the Awesome Ones or, for that matter, of any other energy sources or intelligence."

Very few people hold the mindset that Autists assist humanity in this spiritual evolution. Many may work with Autists, such as parents, caregivers, allies, and friends, but that doesn't mean they believe that Autists help humanity. The Autists can help people in their spiritual evolution; however, they devote their energy to working with *those open to their work*.

Daniel shares, "The Autists focus on helping people where they can get the biggest bang!"

They will focus their energy on those who want to work with them. They can "support the energetic changes going on behind the scenes even if those beings do not know the Autists." If you want the support of the Autists, call upon them with an open heart and mind.

Autists will not work with those people who believe they are damaged humans.

LYRICA'S SPIRITUAL EMBODIMENT

Lyrica Marquez, an Ethereal Autist and one of the inspirations for *The Unsuspected Heroes,* has been working on her spiritual embodiment for decades. During this ascension process, she has teetered with death on more than one occasion. Lyrica understands the importance of integrating her higher spiritual self into her physical form. Yet, as a high vibrational being, there must be a delicate balance in how much and how fast Lyrica can embody, as it could kill her.

Mother Mary likened this process to polarity integration. Embodiment is when the higher self joins in physical form while retaining the connection with her higher self. She said, "Humans absolutely can embody and carry that same energetic frequency (as their higher self)." Meaning that humans do not have the same risks when embodying as an Ethereal Autist would have.

By standing in one's Truth and being authentic, humanity can embody their higher self in physicality and carry the energetic frequency that benefits humanity. The blending or integration of the higher self with the physical, the New Earth experience, impacts others around them in subtle yet profound ways.

CHAPTER 15:

The Autist Collective

The Autist Collective is a group of "silent"
heroes ushering in the New Earth and shed-
ding light for humanity to witness this birthing
and reveal how genuinely divine you are.
—Connie

A GROUP OF ETHEREAL AUTISTS work around the planet
to awaken humanity. That group is called the Autist Collective.

One of the gifts of the Ethereal Autists is their ability *not*
to judge, which is needed to do the work the Autists are doing.
Humanity permits its emotions to cloud its judgment and
labels situations as "good" or "bad" or "right" or "wrong." To do

the energetic work the Autists need to accomplish, they *must* be nonjudgmental.

The Autists hold a larger vision of what can be for humanity. Keep in mind that everything is energy, even the vision. The Autists work with the energy and continue to manipulate, weave, and form situations, circumstances, and events to awaken humanity. Nevertheless, while the Autists hold the vision of a "more significant impression of what can be for humanity, it is up to humankind to move with it," Daniel said. "We hold the construct and infrastructure of the New Earth."

Humanity needs to move with the energy, knowledge, and expectation that the New Earth is already here. It is *our* choice to experience it. We can't wait for someone else to step in and save us. We are the saviors; we need to find it within ourselves, and when awakening, we assist others energetically.

Daniel says, "The Ethereal Autists are far beyond Earth. We are aware of other planets and galaxies, and our awareness and expressions are stronger there than they are here in the physical form on Earth."

As described earlier, the Autists are not wholly in their physical bodies; they have a galactic expression far more powerful than the body we see on Earth. Most of their life essence is elsewhere, as these higher vibrational beings would damage their bodies if they were to embody completely.

Daniel shared that the Autists hold "a hologenetic expression of the New Earth."

Hologenesis is a theory of evolution in which a species divides into two, yet only one thrives. This concept is consistent with other messages suggesting that those experiencing the New Earth will have more ease and grace. At the same time, those remaining in the third dimension will continue with their trials and tribulations.

Daniel said that the Autists are making connections "with a blueprint that is far greater than anything perceived currently within the human consciousness."

When asking what he meant by this, he shared, "What if there were a blueprint for creating a community, and all facets of it were well thought out?" He said that we'd start with the infrastructure and that "humanity is now becoming aware of a New Earth, and within that, they *assume* that they know what it is, *but it is far greater!*"

We have no concept of the sheer magnificence of the New Earth.

Daniel also shared that the Ethereal Autists work with holographic energies given to them by aspects of themselves. In other words, other multidimensional expressions of themselves described as "many different beings from other galaxies and universes" gave the Autists the energy. "It is a hologram projected out."

The Ethereal Autists' energy work to construct this ever-evolving New Earth is beyond our understanding. It involves sacred geometries dealing with Light, Void, and God Code.

Daniel shares, "Humanity's perspective is limited to what it has seen or knows or is in a genetic code at that period."

If we don't have an understanding of something, our brains can't fully process it. The most straightforward example of this would be a human running a four-minute mile. The four-minute barrier broke in 1954. It wasn't considered humanly possible at one time, but today it is the standard for male professional middle-distance runners. Our perceptions of anything are limited by what we have seen or experienced.

Humanity is now shifting into the New Earth. Some may understand that there is something more significant beyond the third dimension, but they cannot perceive it because they still work with third-dimensional foundational pieces. "The New Earth must unfold slowly. There are technologies, skills, and abilities that are not yet perceived within humanity as a whole but are very natural to humankind. They have just not experienced it."

Daniel shared that not all Ethereal Autists in the Autist Collective are doing the God Code work at the same time, but they all hold unique gifts.

The Autist Collective is like a beehive. They move, shift, and communicate rapidly within different galaxies and universes simultaneously. Contrary to how most humanity perceives autistics, they are far from limited.

"We can change the perspective, the dynamics, the energy as needed to continue to hold and build this New Earth hologram. It is much more complex, not just energy in itself. We are vast, and we are many."

When I asked Daniel what his role was in the Autist Collective, relating to the New Earth, he shared, "I am the orchestrator."

Daniel makes sure that the energies that need to move and shift actually occur. He connects with and directs other beings that work with him. These may be other Autists, other Autist Collective members, as well as Guides or Guardians.

When asking about the Guides or Guardians, he typed, "Know that they are ancient galactic warriors, that is all."

Daniel referred to his teammates as one pod and explained that there are many teams or many pods.

"I can hold myself still enough to see multiple pods working at any given point in time and can relay what is needed." Simultaneously, Daniel protects the work and pods. "Although I do not have to do it by myself, I have to keep my awareness open and free. This is my gift, and this is what I can do with these various pods. We discussed one pod, but many pods are going on simultaneously. And, it is not just here on Earth."

I asked Daniel if the pods he mentioned were associated with the Galactic Suns and Susan Oros's work. He answered, "Yes, this is part of the tip. There are more beneath that and around that, but the concept is correct."

He shared that there are more groups throughout this universe. As the Autist Collective gets stronger, other pods awaken, and "humans" in the third dimension who can hold and integrate the energies of the Autists will also awaken and work within a pod.

"So, it is a very prominent time for the Autists to awaken," Daniel said, "to do the work that we have come here to do."

SUSAN OROS'S WORK WITH
THE GALACTIC SUNS

Having mentioned the Galactic Suns and Susan Oros, allow me to give you a "readers digest" version of this work. Susan is the mother of Sammie, a high-vibrational Ethereal Autist. They are the pioneers of this work. Susan writes about it on their site (www.moonoros.one) and in a chapter of *Evolutionary Healer: Radical Wisdom from 18 Ascending Visionaries* by Ariadne Avalon.

The Galactic Suns are one of the first emanations of Source Energy. You may think about it as Source's (God's) first exhale. In that first exhalation, many lineages of Great Beings may be considered the first Soul expression, the twelve Galactic Suns, the Council of Twelve, or the One. Within the first emanation are twelve languages of Source connected to all manifestations of Creation.

Thirty-six Autist Avatars walk the planet today, forming twelve triads (a.k.a. twelve Galactic Suns). For each Galactic Sun, three Autist Avatars form a triad, representing a Sun or Sol (Soul). In other words, each triad is a Galactic Sun. I believe this is the "tip" Daniel refers to in the previous section.

Thousands of Autists around the planet form an Autist Collective working with the twelve triads to heal, reweave, and teach about humanity's Divine Nature and what it means to be part of *all that is.*

As I understand it, Daniel is one of the three Autist Avatars associated with the tenth Galactic Sun.

THE CELLULAR SENTRY OF THE UNIVERSE

When I first began gathering information for *The Unsuspected Heroes,* I sent Connie a list of questions to ask Daniel.

As I drafted my email, an odd thing happened. The first question I typed came out of nowhere, and it wasn't on my notepad. The question was, "Is Daniel St. Germaine?"

Today, I realize how human that question is. We humans are so interested in putting names, titles, and numbers on things. In any case, I sent the email, and this was Connie's response.

"It is interesting that you asked this question. When we were in Sedona last year, Daniel indicated that Lady Portia was his twin flame. I later learned that Lady Portia is the twin flame of St. Germaine.

"I asked Daniel if he was St. Germaine. He hesitantly responded, "no," and then he typed:

"What's important about me is not who
I am, where I am from, how I operate,
or why I am here. The most important
aspect I hold is what I know. At every
moment, I know about the cellular
program of the entire Universe. I am
a cellular sentry of the Universe.
Inviting you to tune into that dimension of me for more explanation."

I wish I could say that I tuned in back then and got a better explanation. But the simple truth is that while I consider myself intuitive, I didn't trust myself with this material. So, when the opportunity arose to inquire about it, I explored it in a session.

In one channeling, when Daniel showed up, I asked, "You once told me that you were a cellular sentry of the Universe. What do you mean by that, and is it related to your role in orchestrating the energy going to the New Earth's holographic expression?"

"It is that and more. Holographically, I can go into time-space dimensions and perceive, modify, exchange, resonate, become one with, and come back out and remain a singular awareness.

"I can merge within those holographic universes, experiences, parallel lifetimes, space-time dimensions, and I can become it and merge with it, but then I can come back singularly in the awareness of who and what I am at this point

(Daniel). I can become one and many, and I can become one in singular focus."

The fourth-dimensional space is space-time. Space-time combines the three dimensions of space (up and down, left and right, forward and backward) with one dimension of time. If we were to pierce the veil of consciousness, time-space would be our experience rather than space-time. We would experience three dimensions of time simultaneously, the past, present, and future, and one dimension of space (yourself).

Daniel can travel in space-time and time-space and manipulate, resonate, and become one with any energetic expression while remaining "Daniel." He merges with these other universes, lifetimes, parallel lifetimes, and can become them. He can become one individual, many individuals, and even speak as a group with a singular voice, similar to how Cerian speaks as a single voice for a collective.

To say that Daniel has had our group playing mental gymnastics as I have attempted to sort out some of his previous lives is an understatement, as he can essentially be anyone and everyone.

CHAPTER 16:

Tough Love

God whispers in your soul and speaks to your heart.
Sometimes when you don't have time to listen,
God has to throw a brick at you. It's your choice:
listen to the whisper—or wait for the brick.
—Unknown

I LOVE THE ABOVE PASSAGE because it is so indicative of
how the Universe speaks to us. If we ignore what God or Source
is telling us, then the bricks do come. I know because I've had
my fair share of bruises along the way.

This warning system happens to all of us as well as humanity as a whole. Let's face it, humankind hasn't made some good
choices, and even with warnings, some things still haven't
changed. As children, when we made poor choices, our

parents likely executed tough love situations. Do you think the Universe is different?

Our current systems, the principles, and the procedures through which things are accomplished must change. Those systems won't make it to the New Earth. They have been breaking, and humanity uses Band-Aids to repair them, but the simple truth is that they will fail and need to be created anew, as we cannot build upon a faulty foundation. The new systems must support all of humanity, not just a specific portion of the population.

I asked Daniel if the Autist Collective intentionally orchestrates tough love situations to demonstrate that the existing ones don't work.

"Not so much intentionally," he began. "It is just by the very nature of beingness that these (tough love situations) will unfold and demonstrate that the systems do not currently work. It is not intended to reveal anything; it is about BE-ING, and by simply *being*, the Autists can demonstrate that it doesn't work."

SYSTEMS WILL CRUMBLE

The systems will fail, and truths will come to the forefront. Daniel spoke about many of these systems.

IT IS TIME FOR A WHOLE NEW EDUCATIONAL PROGRAM.

We currently see the education system shifting. According to Daniel, "It is time for a whole new educational program." It should not be a path of primary education to get a job to make money to retire one day. "This sounds mundane. Things must be observed. Things will happen much quicker. There is not a singular path. People will need to continually shift and upgrade and work on different and new skills."

The information taught to the children currently must change because much of it is no longer valid. There are different generations of children, some now adults, who have embodied to assist humanity's spiritual evolution. These individuals may be called the New Children. The New Children learn differently, and much is absorbed through observation. They are the Indigo Children, Crystal Children, Rainbow Children, and Diamond Children. They are also starseeds.

The educational system shouldn't be a one-size-fits-all program. Once the current educational system adjusts, which won't occur overnight, and likely the changes will come through adult New Children, the children will learn quicker than they have historically. The New Children will continually experience DNA upgrades and develop skills that we today may only imagine in science fiction and visionary literature and films. Many of the New Children are Pure Autists.

TECHNOLOGY IS AWARE AND CONSCIOUS.

New technology is coming. Humanity is beginning to accept and use technology in innovative ways, and humanity's awareness of it and expansion of what it can do is significant. Daniel said that this awareness is "both good and bad."

It is unusual for him to say anything is good or bad because that is judgment. Still, he explained what he meant by bad.

"The Autists hold onto the hologram (of the New Earth) for humanity. The *bad* is that humankind will make some mistakes with technology that could be called harmful, but ultimately, the Earth will get to the holographic New Earth. Technology will be a key because it is aware and conscious."

THE ECONOMY MUST SHIFT.

Daniel said, "The economy must shift to an equal distribution of wealth. Control and power must return to the masses and not the few."

THE GOVERNMENT IS
ALREADY COMING DOWN.

"This is going to be a potentially grave war because this paradigm (humanity being controlled) has been in place for so long, from the beginning of time."

In the beginning, humanity wanted to be led; to survive, they wanted someone to follow. Humankind followed blindly and became "controlled." Today, as some begin living their blueprint and humankind awakens, these individuals recognize that they can lead themselves far better than giving their power away to a few.

"This will be the biggest schism that will be erupting more over the next several years.

"The government is already coming down; it is going to be more extreme, and then there will be a point where it must come back together again for the betterment of humanity, not just within the United States. As people become aware, they begin to recognize their wholeness, sovereignty, and ability to govern themselves, which, for some, will be terrifying."

PEOPLE WILL REALIZE THEY ARE HEALERS.

People will also realize that they are capable of healing themselves. They'll learn that some natural food sources or substances have healing properties and are natural remedies. These realizations will force pharmaceutical companies to change.

"The families of few are currently driving the pharmaceutical companies to keep humanity downtrodden. The vibrant health will go back to the individual."

Each person will be accountable for their health rather than turning it over to a doctor or a drug.

SYSTEMS THAT DON'T HONOR THE INDIVIDUAL AS A SOVEREIGN BEING WILL FAIL.

All systems that don't honor the individual as a sovereign being will need new creation, not reconstruction. Even relationships will change. People will come together in like-mindedness, and while it is a way down the road, there will not be a delineation of races, sex, or age.

The shift to the New Earth will be a different experience for most. It can't be the same because we are all here with our own purpose, and while they may be similar, they will be different.

Throughout time, humanity has been tribal, meaning like-minded individuals have come together to experience life in smaller, inclusive communities. This desire will increase. As star families begin to identify themselves on Earth, they will come together to enjoy the company of like minds, and new communities will emerge.

THE CALM BEFORE THE STORM

When Daniel came in during one particular channeling, he said, "This is the calm before the storm." This channeling was in late February 2021, during political unrest, a pandemic, and the government threatening mandatory vaccinations. There was also extreme weather and natural disasters around the world. The idea that this was "calm" was a bit disturbing. I could only imagine that more tough love was coming for humankind.

Daniel explained that more division, angst, and fear would usher in significant growth. "Do not be surprised if the media exploits catastrophes that will create more angst, fear, and hatred. Know that this will stir change into rapid change."

He further indicated that humanity believed that the challenging part of COVID-19 was getting under control but cautioned otherwise.

When probing further about the storm, Daniel indicated that the storm was the collapse of all the institutions set in motion based upon unique points in time. It is going to get louder. He stated that it is time to change the institutions, and they can only continue to implode before "they can rebuild themselves."

COVID-19 is opening people's eyes to many systems that don't work. The systems collapsing will happen simultaneously. Some institutions are imploding; others are rebuilding. It is already happening.

The speed at how fast or slow all this occurs depends on people. Daniel stated, "It is crucial to stay in the presence of the self." In other words, don't go into panic or fear mode. How swiftly we move through the storm depends on the energy.

If people see these storm-like events as catalysts for growth and new experiences, the events will be more manageable. Otherwise, if people witness them as chaotic destruction, they'll move into fear, which will be more challenging.

Daniel indicated that if there is a good balance between those remaining calm, recognizing that the systems are changing for humanity's evolution, with those in fear and panic, the institutions shifting will roll out slowly and be less chaotic.

THE MATCH OF ENLIGHTENMENT

"Autists hold the 'match of
enlightenment.' Humans are the gasoline
to get this going. EVERYBODY is the
hand of God that strikes the match.
Eventually, together, humanity
ignites the flame."

—Daniel

Daniel shares that when the Autists weave the energy into the New Earth hologram, the energies begin to shift people's perception and awareness of themselves, their sovereignty, and their connection to Source (God). These individuals begin to see differently and reclaim themselves. They pull away from the norm and try things outside the box. These types of surges, similar to what occurred in the sixties (the civil rights movement, antiwar protests, feminism, gay liberation, the environmental movement, and more), change people and create change in the masses.

The breaking down of the systems is part of this shift in consciousness. It is the bricks of life. It is to awaken humanity to its sovereignty. Do not look at the bricks as being bad. They are the catalysts.

IN CHAOS, BE THE OBSERVER

As I write this book, it would seem that in the outer world, there is much chaos—political, financial, educational, and climatic unrest. I've often thought that chaos precedes change. When I asked Daniel if the chaos precipitates the New Earth, he reminded me that the New Earth is already here.

"It is only in human's perception that there is chaos, for the New Earth already is the hologram. It already exists. Humanity chose to pull itself out and away from natural laws existing in any single or multi-cell organism in the cosmos.

"When humanity realizes they are within the confines of these laws and they open up and work with the natural laws, they will see the chaos settle. The paradigm that humanity has created no longer works and is creating chaos."

The Autists weave the energies in the etheric realms for humanity to experience the energy and pay attention to it.

"As it gets more intense, faster, and stronger, the glass will shatter, as it no longer can sustain the energy coming at it, and that is what's happening now."

During periods of chaos, "Push out more love and kindness and compassion rather than fear and hate."

When people fear things, they become angry; it creates a powerful, destructive force causing much harm. One way to look at situations involving chaos is as an observer.

"Recognize that the chaos is all part of the change. Give thanks that the participants of the chaos are bringing issues to the surface to be seen and experienced rather than letting them bubble within the consciousness or confines of humanity."

Shining light on the shadows brings situations to the surface. These situations need to be seen and healed. We're all on different paths and have different roles in this shift.

- For some, their blueprint, their Truth, may be to instigate situations that spread fear and angst.
- For others, their blueprint and Truth may be to shine their light on these situations to bring them to the surface to see them.
- For some, their blueprint and Truth may be to heal the wounds of the victims.
- For others, their blueprint and Truth may be to stand in peace amid the chaos to provide calmness.

There are numerous blueprints and Truths. Everyone plays a role in this shift, and the most critical message here is to honor everyone's Truth by not judging them.

When observing the chaos, never buy into it, as it will cause more stress and duress for you and others around you who are not participating in it. This impact on others is part of a ripple effect across the media, the nation, and the globe. Recognize the situations with love and compassion, for humankind is changing. As Daniel said, "Humanity is showing its ugly side, a side that has been suppressed and wants to come out that is feeling desperate, alone, concerned, and fearful."

The Autist Collective does not weave the chaos. Daniel added, "We bring the energy to the point where it needs to be. We are holding the hologram and the energies coming in. As systems fail, many people recognize the systems no longer work, and some go to fear, frustration, angst, and rage. Then others believe this is the systems crumbling, and those belief systems no longer hold, demonstrating what has been hiding underneath the surface and what humanity does not want."

Stand in the belief that the systems and institutions no longer serve us and will be created for all humanity. Stand in the role of being an observer, not one of judging, anger, and fear.

Remember that the shift in consciousness is a shift in vibrational frequency from fear to love.

WHY DO BAD THINGS HAPPEN TO GOOD PEOPLE?

Our group came up with this topic through a blind selection, during which Connie, Daniel, and I rated a group of preselected book themes. Daniel rated one subject highly, which was, "Why do bad things happen to good people?" I had placed this topic on the low side of my list because I thought it was for the experience and lessons.

The funny thing is that I thought I'd ask Daniel that question in channeling, and his initial response made me laugh.

Daniel, "Why do bad things happen to good people?"

"Well, first, that would be a judgment," Daniel stated.

He is right. There is no good or bad. Our humanity judges a situation or circumstance as good or bad. I let him continue.

"You are referencing the individual rather than the experience. It's all about experience, and it is a choice. The soul contract was written long ago before it (soul) incarnated into form and chose the parents and people it would be associated with. It is all about creation and learning and growing. It is all about the experience. It has already been written, programmed, and transmitted for the highest and best for that human form's particular experience. So, it is not that it is a *bad* thing.

"If you live forever, you are just inherently picking up a different experience. That experience may be lacking in a previous lifetime or is needed to enhance this particular lifetime. Usually, those experiences are tied, not chronologically, but some experiences need to be overcome to grow. It may be perceived that bad things happen to good people. It is not that, though, because that is a judgment based on a very minute perspective, a very *now* (human) perspective."

Consider that every person has a unique blueprint for this life. Some situations we perceive as harmful or bad may even occur to illuminate the darkness to reveal that humanity has been controlled. Consider for a moment that there are millions of what we call Lightworkers on the planet, and they came here to help humanity heal from fear and ego. They came here to help humanity evolve. For evolution to occur, things need to be broken down, such as the systems.

To me, it is not a stretch that some Lightworkers may have chosen to play a role to help expose that the systems are broken and need replacement. But, also, not all Lightworkers have awakened. Consider the possibilities that some may have come to experience tragedies to help humanity wake up by showing that systems are broken, and we've been controlled.

Could it be that some chose to come and experience COVID-19 and die? Could some have decided to get vaccinated, have an adverse reaction, and perish? Both situations demonstrate harmful outcomes and are perceived as bad. Yet, what if that was their blueprint? What if their experience brings light to some circumstances on the planet that need to change?

Humanity has been in slumber, and because they wanted to be led, they followed the leaders blindly (and still do), not realizing that they surrendered their freedom. Humanity is awakening, although slowly.

Could it be that the deaths from COVID-19 and the vaccinations will expose truths? Absolutely. Consider for a moment that COVID-19 is one of those tough-love situations created to catalyze change. COVID-19 is a modality of evolution. There will be more about COVID-19 in Chapter 27: COVID-19 and Vaccinations.

PART IV

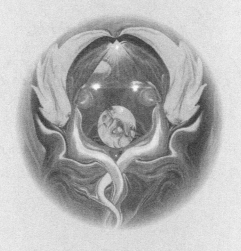

*Lemuria, Atlantis, and
the Magdalenes*

CHAPTER 17:

Energy from Lemuria to Today

We decided to split from Source to experience
Ourselves in magnificence and multitude.
—Mother Mary

PLANETARY GRIDS

SPIRITUAL ENERGY GRIDS, referred to as planetary grids, cover the Earth and hold consciousness for each species, including Earth. They are etheric crystalline structures that some refer to as electromagnetic fields, templates, or matrixes. Drunvalo Melchizedek suggests there are three different planetary grids for humankind: the primal grid, humanity's existing consciousness grid, and the ascension grid, which is called by many names, including the Christ Consciousness Grid.

Humanity's existing consciousness grid is embedded from the first and second to just below the fourth dimension. It regulates electromagnetic systems, such as vortexes and ley lines. It is presently the primary consciousness grid for most of humanity. This grid has a relationship with duality consciousness, where ego and judgment thrive, rather than a relationship with nature. The duality relationship alone certainly explains humanity's carelessness toward our planet.

The primal grid embeds in the first dimension just below the third dimension and holds the consciousness of the original people on Earth, like the Aboriginal people. It was the primary consciousness of our Earth until the flood of Atlantis. The grid has a relationship closer to phi or the golden ratio (golden mean), which links to patterns in nature.

The Christ Consciousness Grid is a synthetic etheric crystalline structure extending from the fourth through the twelfth dimensions. In *The Ancient Secret of the Flower of Life, Volumes I and II*, Drunvalo Melchizedek explains that Ascended Masters Thoth, Araragat, and Ra birthed this grid just before the fall of Atlantis to offer a path for humanity's future ascension, given that humanity's consciousness had fallen. The ascension grid anchors the 5D ascended New Earth consciousness.

Mother Mary shared that polarity is fundamental to the third dimension, which makes sense, given that humanity's primary consciousness grid has a connection with duality. In earlier timelines, in Lemuria, Atlantis, and while the Magdalenes lived, Mother Mary also shared that some people achieved the higher self and physicality's polarity integration. Meaning that individuals in these timelines became aware of who and what they were and "became part of something greater than the planet Earth." In other words, they achieved the union with the I AM presence, integrating their physical and higher self. This is the spiritual and physical integration we seek today.

FROM LEMURIA TO TODAY

Some suggest that Source chose to create us as separate beings so that It (God) could experience physicality. Our experiences are indeed for Source, and each of us is a unique expression of Source, but there is a twist. According to Mother Mary, it was *us* who decided to split from Source to experience Ourselves in magnificence and multitude.

Much of the following information was paraphrased from a channeling with Mother Mary.

The first expression and experience or "step-down" separate from Source was free thought and free choice. Remember that everything is energy, and this first generation from Source was at a high enough vibrational level that it was not in physical form—it was not matter, but it was separate from Source.

On Earth, one can think of that first step-down as the Lemurians. The Lemurians, the ancient pre-Atlantean civilization, were aware of their separation from Source and their blueprint, their purpose, but were not fully developed in physicality.

Over eons, the Lemurians continued to step down in this game of life into physicality, getting denser and denser over time. As they became more physical, their awareness or perception of other time-space dimensions became limited. They went from understanding they were the blueprint and an expression of Source to dipping into matter where they began to experience form but didn't know how to control or create with form. However, they were still more connected to Source than we are today.

Through the cycles of life, the Lemurians became denser. We may think of this as a devolution, but it was an evolution because the intention all along was to become more physical. In the density, they began to lose awareness of their higher self, blueprint, intent, and connection to Source. They forgot about their link to Source.

These cycles began with entering this time-space dimension called Earth, surviving and thriving. We may think of surviving as being able to live and exist. At the same time, thriving meant holding the consciousness in the physical form and continuing the cycles with becoming more physical and forgetting about the Divine Blueprint. This forgetfulness *was* the plan because physicality needed to be experienced and expressed, which meant learning about the body, understanding its workings, determining its primary needs, and prevailing. Genetics and DNA had to continue to grow and evolve.

Through the cycles, humanity lost its awareness of its connection with Source. Mother Mary reminded us that we are here for more than just survival. We are creators and are far greater than our DNA suggests.

Humanity has gone from the Divine Essence and separation into physicality. We forgot that we were part of the Divine expressing physicality. The experiment all along was to see if we would choose to remember, re-member, and integrate the physical with the higher self after forgetting who we were. Our physicality has evolved enough to impact the DNA structure in the stranding, remembering, and awakening of other strands so that the body can perceive and begin to absorb these higher-level energies and awarenesses.

Daniel indicated that our DNA has and continues to change. We have and continue to experience DNA activations throughout the generations. In the ancient Egyptian period, "the DNA at that point was being readied, modified, and activated." During the Jesus or Magdalene timeline, the intention was for humanity to evolve, and even though the events did not occur the way intended, "the DNA was activating and moving forward."

"From the moment we chose to descend into physical form, DNA has been changing and modifying itself. There have been other beings from other planets within and without our galaxy coming in and aiding us." Many would refer to them as aliens or extraterrestrials, but that is not the case. The truth is that humanity comes from Source, the creator of our universe, and the alien species do too.

CHAPTER 18:

Evolution Jumps Triggered by Off-Planet Beings

Do not forget that we are all hybrids,
and it was destined to be so.
—Daniel

THROUGHOUT HUMANKIND'S HISTORY, there were points where evolution jumps needed to occur. These periods included Lemuria, Atlantis (Egypt), and when the Magdalenes walked the Earth. The Magdalenes were a small group of Essenes that included Mary Magdalene, Jesus, Mother Mary, Miriam (Jesus's cousin), Anna (Jesus's grandmother), and many others.

There is an energetic connection between the Ethereal Autists, Lemurians, Atlanteans, and the Magdalenes, and the energetic link has remained throughout time. This energy moves from a very high level of expression (high consciousness) in Lemuria. The energy gets denser and moves into matter (physicality) in Atlantis. While the Magdalenes did their work, the energy began to become less dense. It began moving back toward the higher consciousness and less physicality.

Throughout the specific points in history, this energy from Lemuria connected the flow of spirit and physicality. The energy has always continued and is meant to continue to weave itself together.

The two peoples, the Lemurians and Atlanteans, entwined. They were stepping in and out of each other dimensionally. This entanglement is similar to what is occurring now, with humans residing in the third, fourth, and fifth dimensions. Back then, people were shifting the dimensions also, and some continued to shift into the awareness of their sacredness.

EVOLUTION JUMP DURING YESHUA'S TIME

When asking Cerian if a spiritual evolution jump needed to occur during Jesus's, or Yeshua's, time on the planet, Cerian said, "It was an awareness brought forth again. From physicality, one could experience their higher self, their true and sovereign self. That energy was brought back into humanity's awareness, but did it succeed? No! The energies were available for humanity to access, but too few individuals had achieved this state of integration."

In other words, while the Magdalenes did their work, they had achieved the higher states. Their DNA activated and moved forward through their children, impacting humanity, but that critical mass of awakening we seek today, the hundredth monkey effect, was not reached.

MYSTERY SCHOOLS

Some people, first during the Lemurian era, then Atlantean, and then later, remained connected to their higher self. They remembered who they were and built esoteric schools to remind people of their divinity.

According to Drunvalo Melchizedek, the first mystery school on Earth would have been the Naacal Mystery School taught by Ay and Tiya in Lemuria. This couple instructed how to achieve immortality (ascension) through a form of interdimensional lovemaking. In this practice, there is no touching, no penetration, and when successful, it results in the birth of an immortal child, and the parents achieve immortality.

Another school worthy of mention includes Thoth's Mystery Schools (6000 BC–3000 BC) in Atlantis. Thoth, the author of the *Emerald Tablet*, is also known as the Sumerian god, Ningishzidda. He is an Anunnaki, an off-planet being and the son of Enki and Ereshkigal.

There were off-planet beings, such as Thoth, who came to help humanity remember its divinity. They helped reintroduce that awareness. Sometimes people remembered and could integrate the polarity integration, the spiritual and the physical.

Cerian said, "As the energies began to shift into denser form over thousands of years, the people stopped evolving and were no longer able to communicate with the higher vibrational beings such as Thoth. Many of these beings are still here, but most of humanity is generally unable to communicate with them. As one awakens to their sacred blueprint, they will once again be able to work directly with these Masters."

THE ANUNNAKI: THOSE WHO FROM HEAVEN TO EARTH CAME

At this point in the book, it should not shock you that humans have alien DNA. One of the off-planet influences was the Anunnaki. Much of the information in this section is from Daniel, though it was from earlier dialogues rather than part of the channeling sessions.

Many believe that the Anunnaki are from Nibiru, but according to Daniel, there is more than one Nibiru, supporting a theory that Nibiru is a battlestar, not a planet. He also shared that some of the Anunnaki are from Sirius.

The Anunnaki initially descended to Earth to search for minerals to repair and restore the atmosphere of Nibiru. They are a mix of reptilians (but not Draconian reptilians) and humanoid starseed. When the Anunnaki descended to Earth, there was a king that many today call Anu. Daniel says, "Anu is a title meaning the "most high." It is not a name."

The Anunnaki king was Eretekhan, and he was of a royal humanoid bloodline and had two noteworthy sons. Enlil was Eretekhan's son by his half-sister, Antu, and was of the royal lineage, while Enki was part reptilian, as his mother was the Snake Queen of a separate reptilian civilization. The union between Eretekhan and Antu was political, uniting two royal houses.

However, Enki was always treated as an outcast, even though he was the older son. In contrast, Enlil was, like a military general, placed in charge of Earth and heir to the throne of Earth and Nibiru until another Anunnaki, Marduk, took it by force.

Enki was a geneticist and sent to South Africa, where the Anunnaki mining expedition occurred. Many Anunnaki authorities suggest that Enki and his half-sister, Ninhursag, created humankind to be slaves to mine the ore (gold). According to Daniel, Enki created clones to assist the Anunnaki in their mining. These imperfect ape-men (the clones) were known as Loo Loo Amaloos. Other experiments by the Anunnaki created many different interspecific hybrids, explaining the many mythical crossbreeds found in art and literature (human-goat hybrids, human-bird hybrids, human-fish, and many others).

Later, Enki and his first wife and half-sister, Ninhursag, perfected the modern-day human, but humans were never intended to be slaves. Ninhursag was Enlil's full sister and also of a royal bloodline. Enki combined his genes and a primitive man's genes (Homo erectus ape-man). Ninhursag was impregnated, and she carried and birthed the first human that humankind thinks of today as Adam. As a result, the first man had the DNA of primitive man, alien humanoid, and reptilian.

The first humans were higher-dimensional beings, and Enki wanted to teach them their true nature. Both Eretekhan and Enlil were annoyed by this and told Enki to stop. They wanted humans to evolve on their own rather than use the Anunnaki knowledge and science. Enki's father and brother, and likely the governing council, felt that humankind wasn't ready to remember its divinity.

The council directed Enki and Ninhursag to manipulate the human DNA, and they did. Enki started sneaking humans off to caves to teach them. This likely was the origination of the Brotherhood of the Snake, one of the first mystery schools (approximately 6,000 BC). When Enlil learned about this, he was outraged that humans were given this knowledge and perhaps even jealous that Enki had perfected the creation of humans. Enki was villainized and alienated by his brother. This situation led to conflict among the Anunnaki and, ultimately, a nuclear war.

According to Sumerian text from Mesopotamia, "the collective name of the Elohim is Anunnaki, which is translated as "lofty ones, shining ones, or those who from Heaven to Earth came."[1] Keep in mind that the Sumerian cuneiform tablets predate the Old Testament and many scholars agree that the biblical stories were inspired by ancient Sumerian, Akkadian, Babylonian, and Ugaritic texts.

The Anunnaki are very tall beings. Enki himself was over ten feet in height, and he and other male Anunnaki ("sons of God") had sex with the "daughters of men," their offspring being the Nephilim (plural) and the giants noted in the Hebrew Bible (Genesis 6:4 and Numbers 13:33).

In ancient Egypt (technically Atlantis), the alien influence continued with Thoth (Enki's son), Osiris, Isis, and Horus. The Egyptian gods' teachings continued in the Egyptian Mystery Schools, and Aten (the sun god) communicated with Amenhotep IV or Akhenaten (around 1,300 BC).

According to Daniel, there have been other alien species. Many galaxies, universes, and many "multitudes of sentient beings' consciousnesses" have occurred and had their own evolutionary experiences. "Some are far ahead of us, and some are far behind us; it is all the constant rotation of creation.

---

1   Christine R. Page, *The Healing Power of the Sacred Woman: Health, Creativity, and Fertility for the Soul*, Simon & Schuster 2012.

Even today, many off-planet beings continue to work with and participate with humanity."

Daniel included the Lemurians, Atlanteans, Arcturians, Sirians, Pleiadians, and Anunnaki as off-planet beings that are part of this galaxy and universe. He also said, "Do not forget that we are all hybrids, and it was destined to be so."

CHAPTER 19:

Singular Time-Space versus Dimensions

The fall of consciousness in Atlantis was an experiment to see if, after achieving physicality, humanity would seek its enlightened self in physicality and integrate its Christic Self.
—Daniel

WHILE RESEARCHING the Lemurians and the Atlanteans, some authorities suggest the two types of people were in different dimensions. I was curious about this, so I asked Daniel about it in a session.

LEMURIAN DIMENSIONS

"Daniel, what dimensions were the Lemurians in?" I asked.

"They *are* within *all* dimensions," Daniel shared. "There is a misrepresentation that one must be only in one dimension; this is not true. Dimensions are accessed. It is more important that access is in a time and space."

Daniel continued, "The 'I,' as Daniel, has experienced many dimensions. We can layer it (dimensions) like a cake, assuming that a lower realm has more mass and a higher dimension has less mass, and it is more toward thought.

"The Lemurians were many step-down versions from pure thought. They could descend into matter but chose to live, most likely, from the seventh to the twelfth dimension.

"Many Lemurians continued to experience in *all dimensions,* in one time-space because they could. It was an expression and experience of living, but in a more singular time, a more singular space, which is important, rather than the dimensions.

"What is important is that it is an expression and experience of living in one time-space."

Time-space is where everything happens simultaneously—the past, present, and future (the three dimensions of time). In other words, it was more important the Lemurians be in a physical form in space-time rather than experience all the dimensions. That was the Lemurians' intention, to experience form.

"It happened from the very moment the Lemurians began to experience life within a physicality or more than thought. It was a very gradual descent, so it wasn't just one fall. It was millenniums because physical form became more the objective than the ability to travel through dimensions."

ATLANTEAN DIMENSIONS

"What about the Atlanteans? What dimensions were they in?" I asked.

Daniel replied, "Some Atlanteans were in the same dimensions as the Lemurians, yet most were in the lower realms. The majority were beginning to incorporate themselves into matter. They needed to move into the lower realms of the fifth, fourth, and third dimensions."

You may have heard about the fall of Atlantis. Most associate the fall with the sinking of the land, as a flood and earth changes occurred, but what truly fell was humanity's consciousness. As discussed earlier, the fall in consciousness was gradual, not a sudden plummet from the twelfth dimension in Lemuria to the third dimension in Atlantis (where we are today).

As the Lemurians began to fall to the lower dimensions, they could create and experience more in physicality. They had more impact on creation and life in the physical realms as co-creators. That was the beginning of the fall. As more and more experienced specific frequencies, they began to forget about the higher frequencies. As time passed, their ability to maneuver between dimensions quickly sank, and with that, they kept dropping to lower frequencies.

After hearing that the fall of Atlantis was gradual, I had to probe further. Much information has been channeled suggesting otherwise. I've read theories about the terrible firestone, the Martians, the Aryans, about Marduk and the satellite falling to Earth, and many other suppositions.

"Was there a situation that caused the Atlanteans to plummet? If so, was it intentional and part of the Master Blueprint?" The Master Blueprint is the Prime Creator's plan set at the beginning of the universe's creation for the Earth to ascend to a higher vibration, the New Earth.

"It was a possibility within the blueprint, which became a reality," Daniel said. "It was one of many (realities), but that singular event was not what plummeted humanity. Humanity had already been experiencing more physicality. As the Atlanteans became less aware, they sought more power and control over themselves, their environment, and others.

"That fall was not just one moment in time, it had been happening gradually, and yes, it was supposed to happen. It was part of the evolution of moving consciousness into a lower level of awareness and shifting humanity into the expression of physicality."

Daniel is not saying that the stories of the terrible firestone and others did not happen. He is saying that the fall in consciousness had been happening all along and was the original intent.

"At some point in time, there was a separation," Daniel began. "Some retained memories and were still working in the higher dimensions. They chose to discern themselves and stay in the higher dimensions, while others decided to fall into the physicality and forget their spirituality.

"It is an experiment to see if humanity would seek its enlightened self after achieving physicality and integrate its Christic Self. It was the dumping of spiritual consciousness into humankind to see whether or not humanity would seek its enlightened self, find Itself (Higher Christic Self), and merge into the physical form.

"This is not the first time this has happened for humanity; it is a curve, awareness, awakening, shifting, moving forward, moving back."

This section reminded me of something Cerian had channeled a few years earlier that inspired a chapter in *The Unsuspected Heroes.*

CHAPTER 20:

Cerian on the Humanoid Experiment

When given a choice of playing in the dirty sandbox or seeking out your enlightened self, which path would you choose? In either case, there should be no judgment.

THE FOLLOWING IS REPRINTED with permission from 616 Editions, an Imprint of Jenness, the publisher of *The Unsuspected Heroes*.

I AM CERIAN

Freedom is a privilege. You are a participant in the Humanoid Experiment. You chose to participate in an experiment; only you do not remember. You knew you wouldn't be able to recall any of this, but it was such a unique game and test, and everyone wanted to join in.

The humanoid DNA was manipulated on more than one occasion. On Earth, many blame the Anunnaki for this, and they did re-engineer it. However, DNA manipulation began before even Tiamat, all the way back to the beginning of your universe's creation. (Note: Tiamat is a planet pulverized during the Anunnaki-Reptilian wars, and half of the planet became fragmented, remaining in the asteroid belt. The other half exists today as Earth.)

While this may sound harsh, this dismantling of the DNA was intentional; to make the ascension of humanity *nearly* unachievable.

This *was* the Divine Plan.

This *was* part of the Master Blueprint of the Humanoid Expression in your universe.

139

This *is* the foundation for the human story—the greatest experiment in all worlds.

What I ask at this moment is that you absorb this and know this in your being. You signed up and chose this. There is no one to blame. Here are fundamental Truths you have failed to remember.

Source, or what you would call God, created every soul as a step-down version of Itself to experience more of Itself, and every soul is Divine. Source created light so that It could truly discern darkness by experiencing its polarity.

Each human soul is pure Christ Consciousness, is perfect, Divine, and whole in every way, only it does not remember.

What is the Humanoid Experiment?

What if Pure Consciousness, that God-awareness was separated from matter intentionally, from Its being, but It remains intact, complete with the remembrance of Its Pure Consciousness at Its Higher Soul or Higher Self?

What if the lower self, the lower consciousness, had a veil obscuring that It is Divine and given free will to choose whether it would follow a light path or a dark path?

How would existence now manifest? How would it create? Because all souls are creators, and they are here to create. Would the consciousness seek its Higher Self, its Pure Consciousness? Would it seek out its stabilization, its polarity integration, or would it pursue power? Would it strive for control? Manipulation? Or beauty, love, and harmony?

Is it not a grander story to have consciousness awaken Itself and realize Itself and Its capabilities again? Isn't that a more meaningful story? That was always the hypothesis, and humankind is an experiment.

The game moderators, beings from different galaxies, and universes developed and implemented the Master Blueprint of the universe. They were invited to participate in the game throughout time. Though you sometimes refer to some of its members as the Brotherhood & Sisterhood of Light (formerly known as the Great White Brotherhood), they are the Cosmic Council. These members were invited to fully participate and incarnate throughout time with one caveat: like you, they needed to forget who they are, and they needed to play on both sides of the spectrum, the light, and the dark. Most of these Ascended Masters found their way back to their Higher Selves, and their mission remains to assist in the spiritual evolution of the planet's occupants. However, other game moderators never made it back to the light and became lost in power and control and remain today a threat to humankind and a menace to the game.

Remember that freedom is a privilege, this is an experiment, and *the time has come to awaken to the Truth about who you are.*

I am Cerian

To me, Cerian's discussion of the Humanoid Experiment is the same experiment Daniel refers to in the earlier chapter. Our lives are part of some elaborate game to see if we awaken. There is a veil obscuring who we are, meaning God. When given a choice to play in the dirty sandbox or seek out our enlightened self, which path will we choose? Will we opt for the unification of the higher self in physical form? Or choose to remain in physicality, which was the Lemurian intention all along?

It is a choice, and given that we are sovereign beings and get to choose, there should be no judgment in either case.

CHAPTER 21:

Anasazi and Mayans

The templates are here. They must be remem-
bered. That is why we say what was old
is now new, and what is new is old.
—Daniel

I'VE ALWAYS BEEN INTRIGUED by the disappearing ancient civilizations, from the very, very old in Turkey (*Göbekli Tepe, Catalhöyük*) to the more recent Machu Picchu in Peru and the Anasazi in the four corners area of the United States (Arizona, Colorado, New Mexico, Utah). I have visited many Anasazi and Inca civilization ruins.

All over the world, ancient cultures popped up and disappeared; their fates remain a mystery. Archeologists have speculated their demise as natural catastrophes, wars, pestilence, famine, or depopulation, but they aren't sure in most cases.

In one of Dolores Cannon's *The Convoluted Universe* books, she uncovered that many of these civilizations were experiments. The individuals incarnated in the ancient civilizations were embodiments of a very high-level soul. To explain what I mean by high-level, I need to remind you that you and I are fractals, or step-down versions, of Source. There are multiple levels between ourselves and Source. The high-level soul would be one of the earliest step-downs from Source.

In Cannon's research, she suggested that the people in some disappearing cultures were embodiments of one high-level soul. This soul had multiple manifestations in these cultures. The civilizations were away from other cultures, so they weren't influenced by others. According to Cannon's work, they practiced mass ascensions.

When given the opportunity, I inquired with Daniel about this theory in a channeling. He agreed that the people were embodiments of a high-level soul.

"Daniel, was it an experiment, and did it leave a sort of template here for the future ascension?" I asked. Think of a template as a blueprint; it governs the form of something. In this case, a template or blueprint holds the plan of the evolved human.

"That is accurate," Daniel began. "But the templates *are* here. They must be remembered, and that is why we say what was *old is now new, and what is new is old.*"

"Is it true that at least one person who experienced an ancient mass ascension has returned to the planet?" I asked. "And do they walk among humanity to assist with the ascension?"

"They never really left. Let's put it this way—the consciousness does not leave. The physicality may return to dust, and the consciousness may choose to re-embody again into physical or material form at any given point in time. So yes, that is accurate. Consciousness never left. It was continually monitoring, paying attention, and choosing wisely when to come back into form. There is a big difference here."

After Connie transcribed the channeling and Daniel graded it, he typed out:

"This is a form of reincarnation. I'd like you to contemplate this. Reincarnation just doesn't happen in the physical body."

Reincarnation, the continuation of a soul in a new form, is not limited to a body. In this case, Daniel suggests that consciousness, which is energy, never leaves and remains on the planet. When we have physical experiences and die, our spark of life will return to the soul, but the consciousness remains and can embody in physical form at any point.

Connie messaged during this part of the channeling, "Daniel would like this particular point overemphasized, 'the old is now new, and what is new is old.'"

In a subsequent session, I asked Daniel to help me flesh out this concept, and the following information came through.

"When the soul reincarnates," Daniel began, "it is an old soul, and it is new. It is very new at that moment in reincarnation whether the consciousness is in the body or not.

"There is a cyclical aspect of life, and it helps us flow with it when thinking that something old is new. When experiencing something new, it means one cycle has ended while another has begun. Our lives consist of millions of cycles in a lifetime. One can experience thousands of endings in one day. We don't realize the countless beginnings and endings each day.

"These cycles are a way to jump from linear time to no time. (The God aspect of you is timeless.) The sequences put you in a space between the physical plane of existence in this space-time continuum and where beginnings and endings don't even exist.

"This practice of 'the old is new, and the new is old' puts you in between and makes you unique. Having a perception like this builds bridges of consciousness that exist outside this planet."

I asked Cerian about this concept, and they added, "The soul comes into a physical expression. It has experienced many lives before, though not in this particular physical form. This physical form experiences this singular life, and when it completes its life experience, the soul goes back to pure energy or consciousness, having no form. There is the death of body and birth into pureness, of no time, no space. This cycle repeats over and over. Birth into physical form, death to pure consciousness; death of physical form, birth into pure consciousness."

PART V

*Ruffling Feathers and
Rattling Cages*

CHAPTER 22:

Multidimensionality 101

Unlimited events occur in alternate realities to maximize our experience of life, which is why we are here—to experience.

ARE THERE PAST LIVES?

PAST LIVES MAY SEEM elementary for this book; however, hang with me for a moment. While many psychics and an Ethereal Autist have told me about some of my past lives, I have zero recall of those lives. I wasn't wholly sold about them.

I had conjured up an idea that while "Alex" was a unique expression of a soul having multiple experiences, I pondered that "Alex" was a "one and done." In other words, when I left, my experiences would return to the soul, but "Alex" would never return for another lifetime.

In a channeling session, Daniel confirmed that there are such things as past and future lives, but "Alex" was indeed "one unique expression of her soul." When a person's life is over, their spark of life and experiences return to the soul or higher self. The individual whose life is over "continues to be a fractal of its original expression (its soul) and adds to (absorbs) and is part of that expression of that soul experience of creation."

In my case, "Alex" would not come back in another life or another expression of "Alex." The soul comes back to experience a new life, in a new spark, and the new entity may have a memory of "Alex," but it is that unique expression of "Alex" that is *one and done*, and it lives within the experience of the soul.

"Alex" does not have past lives. "Alex's" *soul* has past and future lives. The experiences of "Alex" return to the soul, and memories of "Alex" may or may not be experienced by my soul's other expressions or lives.

THE SOUL AND THE SPARK OF LIFE

Humans are multidimensional. They have other incarnations, other lives, in different dimensions, at the same time. Only they are not aware of them and don't realize their physical experiences are illusionary. The simultaneous lives are considered different expressions of the person.

An individual (the self) is a physical expression of a soul. Humans have a spark of life that is an aspect of the soul "within," though not within the physical body. There are three bodies in yogic and Vedantic philosophy: the physical, astral, and causal body. According to yogic belief, the causal body contains the soul and is the most subtle body, and it is within the other two bodies.

The soul is also called the higher self and is part of a soul group.

One can think of the soul group as a point linking the multiple sparks of life of that soul (or its other multidimensional lives from various incarnations). It is consciousness coming back to itself in different expressions and forms.

Physical Expression of a Soul = Self

Spark of Life = Aspect of the Soul

Soul = Higher Self = Aspect of a Soul Group

Soul Group = Point Connecting Other
Multidimensional Expressions of *Itself*

Soul or Soul Group is Multidimensional

MULTIDIMENSIONALITY

Multidimensionality is a consciousness with numerous expressions (selves) that are uniquely independent and separate in thought and sometimes physicality. Not all expressions are in physical form. Each expression is a singular focal point (or a higher soul awareness).

The soul and soul group is multidimensional, not the self. Daniel says the soul or soul group is a "multidimensional individual experiencing life, awareness, and expression in different time-space dimensions simultaneously."

These multidimensional expressions include our past, future, and present lives. Moreover, these expressions can be human, alien, angelic, elemental, animal, and even matter.

The self is typically unaware of its multidimensional experiences, but the higher self and the soul group are aware. Daniel further expanded that while an individual may remember the other multidimensional expressions going through this ascension, it only will occur if it is part of the individual's blueprint, which relates to what the self is to learn while they are here.

As mentioned earlier, words fail to describe the endless levels and layers between the self and Source. These layers go beyond the spark of life, soul, soul group, etc. Daniel suggested that we "think of it all as ONE." Consider for a moment that there is one soul, and that is the Oversoul. The

Oversoul is the unity of all souls that transcends all individual consciousnesses.

While we have this insistent need to understand and put things in some hierarchy, from the self to Source is one energy, and all its levels combined are one and whole, and that is Oneness.

THE SOUL IS MULTIDIMENSIONAL

You are indeed a unique expression, and within you have a divine spark of your soul. When your physical body dies, this spark returns to your soul or your higher self.

You are a spiritual being having a physical experience, but at the soul level, you are not physical and could even suggest that physicality is an illusion. What is true is that your soul (not you) has multiple experiences simultaneously in other realms or dimensions. Some of these experiences are in the physical, and others are in the ethereal realms. Your soul may even have different experiences on Earth at the same time. Some refer to this as split incarnations, parallel incarnations, or soul splits, which is unlike a twin soul. In the latter case, the masculine and feminine division creates two souls with their own unique experiences.

What does all this mean? It is possible, yet not probable, to meet another expression of your soul. Perhaps this knowledge sheds some light on the Golden Rule, *treat others the way you like to be treated* (because you never know when you'll meet your "self").

PARALLEL LIVES OR ALTERNATE DIMENSIONS

Within our physical experience in the third dimension, we have unlimited alternate dimensional experiences, which many refer to as parallel lives. These existences would be where our doppelgangers hang "our" hats.

Essentially, any time we put energy into choosing something, we create different realities. For example, perhaps in high school, you contemplated becoming a police officer or a social worker. Before deciding, you weighed your options and became a social worker. In some other dimension, however, you became a police officer. Which one is real? They are both real.

This phenomenon alone can mean there are many truths. For example, in one reality, the Master Jesus may have died on a cross and resurrected in three days. In another reality, he survived the crucifixion, had a family, and ascended to the higher dimensions.

These alternate or parallel realities offer unlimited events to maximize our experience of life, which is why we are here—to experience.

TIMELINES CONVERGING

Have you had an experience where something in your world suddenly wasn't what you remember? Perhaps the name of something is spelled differently, or lines in a movie changed. Or you remember the names of products differently. Other common examples are cartoon characters, car designs, or logo changes. While psychologists may refer to this as false memory syndrome (FMS), others may call it a Mandela effect.

Fiona Broom thought up the term "Mandela effect" when she and others remembered that Nelson Mandela had died in the 1980s while in prison, not in 2013. Connie is one who clearly remembers Mandela's death in the eighties and how her family mourned his passing.

I read someplace the timelines were converging. When I say timelines, I mean alternate or parallel dimensions. I wondered if this phenomenon could explain false memory or the Mandela effect.

Daniel broached the subject in a channeling. "Humanity is being able to witness, experience, and be aware of this (timeline convergence) energetically." Our participation in this "allows humanity to resonate in a manner that they have not been able to before because they are acknowledging it (the Mandela effect), they are aware of it, participating in it, and engaging with it. This changes the energies and the convergence entirely."

As we recognize the differences, or Mandela effects, and talk about them, we change the energy and somehow impact

the convergence. Daniel also added that the "great convergence" was causing a lot of sleeping difficulties.

Our higher self is actively engaged at night, and consequently, the physical form has a restless sleep rather than the
deep sleep one typically experiences.

Daniel shared more on why the convergence is causing
sleep difficulties.

"It is also primal. It goes back
to being on high alert. The body
wakes up as a means of more physical
participation.

"The effects of sleep deprivation on a
human are profound. The great convergence on a micro level is one thing,
and on a macro level (depending on
the individual) will have a dramatic
difference. Depending on your level
of sensitivity, you will have sleep
problems. This convergence is why a
large majority of us Autists have
sleep issues."

CHAPTER 23:

My New Thought Concepts Challenged

It is not that the Autists are higher dimensional beings. They are all-dimensional beings.

THE PEOPLE WHO BUILD HOUSES DO NOT CREATE THEM.

DURING THIS PROJECT, Connie and I generated questions for the channelings. Admittedly, I had certain expectations going in. I'd write queries and expect the answers to align with my research and beliefs. But, gosh, I was *so* wrong. Instead, the dialogues surprised me, even pinning Mother Mary against Daniel, from which a lively discussion ensued.

During one discussion with Mother Mary in channeling, I asked, "Is the following statement true or false—All humans are creators?" I was expecting "yes."

Mother Mary said, "This is true."

After the channeling was transcribed and ran past Daniel, he disagreed and typed:

> "This is NOT true. Not all humans have the capacity to be creators, as that is not their role. All humans have access to God-consciousness, but not all access this God-consciousness. There is a difference. The difference is profoundly significant. The people who build houses do not create them."

So, I thought, *What am I supposed to do with this?* I sent Connie a message to ask Daniel, "Is Daniel including the backfill people that I often refer to as AI, as humans?"

A note from Connie said, "Daniel did clarify that he was including backfill and AI with humanity."

Please have patience with me here. I will get to the backfill people and AI.

THERE ARE WEEDS IN THIS BEAUTIFUL
GARDEN THAT NEED PLUCKING.

My discussion with Mother Mary continued, "Is this true or false—All humans are Source (God) Energy?"

Again, Mother Mary agreed, but Daniel added:

```
"This is not a simple true and false
question. All humans are Source Energy
if they choose to be, but it is false
because some don't choose that. Not
even Source can impose upon anyone's
free will. Free will is a very power-
ful thing. This is why Autists cannot
do all the work for humanity because
it is humanity's free will to make
changes."
```

Back to Mother Mary, I asked, "All humans are here with a higher purpose or blueprint. True or false?"

"Yes, this is true," Mother Mary said.

Again, after the session and the transcription, Connie writes, "Daniel says *no* again. I think it's because not all humans are supposed to ascend." She added her thoughts, "I disagree that all humans have a higher purpose. It is a little too kumbaya to me. We all come from the *same* Creator, and that Creator is both good, bad, and in between. Thus, all of Its creations do not have a higher purpose unless you consider that higher purpose can be evil. Am I looking at the higher purpose statement in too much of a human fashion? *I believe there are weeds in this beautiful garden that need plucking.* Otherwise, they impact us all."

I wondered if, again, Daniel was considering AI or backfill people. I also believed that if an individual's blueprint were to be a weed, that'd be that individual's higher purpose. So, I sent a message to Connie to ask Daniel, "Is this true or false—All *humans* are here with a purpose or blueprint." I intentionally omitted *higher* in "higher purpose."

"This is very true," he typed.

WE WERE NEVER GIVEN THE FINE PRINT.

I had believed that we are all creators, first in thought (mind), then in form. I'd also believed we are all Source energy, and we're all here with a higher purpose. Daniel rattled my cage.

One more question to ask Mother Mary before I expand on these dialogues. "Is this statement true or false: Life is a game, and we all agreed to play?"

"This is true," Mother Mary said.

After the transcription, Connie writes, "Daniel rated this a two." This rating would mean that 20 percent of the response is correct.

Daniel typed:

"Life is a game. Not everybody agreed to play this game. We were never given the FINE PRINT.

It CANNOT be stated that humanity
agreed to play because there is an
element of deception against some of
humanity. Although not ALL agreed to
play, most did. Those who disagreed
are in a form of slavery."

I messaged Daniel and asked, "Is it true that those playing
the game in the capacity of being an antagonist or adversary
may have that in their blueprint (purpose)?"

Daniel typed, "True."

If an individual's purpose in the game is to be an adversary
or a weed, that is their purpose or blueprint. It is our humanity
that judges the mission of being a weed as being "less than."

Autists have access to all dimensions. At one point in the
interactions between Mother Mary's answers and Daniel's
grading, he typed something very interesting. First, he graded
a message from Mother Mary as being inaccurate, then added:

"This is not criticism. Please know
that Mother Mary is very human, even
in the ascended state. In these
realms, there is a lot that is missed,
even after the ascension."

It was fascinating that he was not addressing Rasew or
Shauna, the channel, as being inaccurate. Instead, he was

suggesting that Mother Mary herself was wrong. This pushed my buttons a bit. Mother Mary has always been my "go-to" saint or Ascended Master when seeking guidance. Now, Daniel suggested that she had limitations.

Yet, I have been on the path with the Ethereal Autists for some time. The Autists are closer to Source, meaning they are one of the early generations or step-down versions of Source or God. When one of them communicates, I listen.

Daniel continued,

> "Twelfth dimensional Mother Mary is not perfect, and that is okay. Even in her ascended state, she is human, and as a human, she has a lower self."

Keep in mind that we are all multidimensional. The Ascended Masters may access the sixth through twelfth dimensions. Cerian, the collective in which Daniel and Shauna both have expressions, is in the sixteenth dimension.

I also take my job seriously to seek the Truth, and I realize that not everyone knows or believes that many Autists are higher spiritual beings. I thought this response was an opportunity to help explain why I place credence in Daniel's answer over Mother Mary's.

"Daniel, for the readers to understand why you can access the information more accurately, is it because the Autists are in higher dimensions than the Ascended Masters?"

"We, Autists, have access to *all* dimensions. It is not about the Autists being higher or lower. It is frequency / energy / consciousness-based.

"All the dimensions are connected. There is this point of intersection for all dimensions, which makes astral traveling easy. Think of it as one dimension. One can free oneself of the idea of lower or higher dimensions.

"Seeing dimensions as higher or lower serve their purpose for teaching here on Earth to give the idea that one must be at certain frequencies to access dimensions. But the whole of it is when you get beyond Christ Consciousness and can access anything you want; that is when the higher and lower idea of dimensionality means nothing anymore. It is not about higher or lower, as it limits the idea of multidimensionality."

It is not that the Ethereal Autists are higher dimensional beings. They are *all*-dimensional beings. Experiencing higher dimensions may serve us on Earth, but that is not the case in the New Earth and higher realms.

We are all fractals of Source Energy. The Ethereal Autists can access information more readily than the Masters, yet some Ascended Masters are likely other expressions of the Pure Autists. Even consider the possibility that *you* are an expression of a Master embodied to fulfill your spiritual blueprint.

In any case, much of this information conflicted with my New Thought research. I am reminded of what Leilah, my Autist friend, has said, "Forget everything you've ever been taught."

I will explore artificial intelligence (AI), backdrop or back-fill people, and this game of life in the pages to follow.

CHAPTER 24:

The Backdrop People, AI, and Starseeds

Forget everything you've ever been taught.
—Leilah, Ethereal Autist

I BECAME FAMILIAR WITH THE CONCEPT of the backdrop people through Dolores Cannon's work. Since that time, I've also heard people refer to it as backfill or background people. Cannon was a teacher of a hypnosis method called Quantum Healing Hypnosis Technique (QHHT). It permitted the practitioner to communicate with the subconscious, whom Cannon believed to be the Higher Self or Oversoul.

Cannon spent almost fifty years hypnotizing people, at first mainly to teach about reincarnation, but her work expanded into much more fringe research later in her life. She suggests that we create the people in our background. We create our world, and people play various roles in our lives. She said the superfluous people we see throughout life are "extras" in our movie. They are not real and are soulless. She indicated that they are strictly energy and a hologram.

She suggested that each person is the creator of their reality, and it is all illusion. Each is the leading actor, screenwriter, and director. Cannon further indicated that the prominent people, the costars, in our lives are real. In contrast, the extras in the background are on a different evolutionary path than humanity.

MY MOVIE, MY COSTARS, AND EXTRAS

As I wrote this chapter, I recalled an experience I had as a very young child—perhaps three or four years of age. I was with my family, and looking around at them, I had an overwhelming feeling that one day when my life was over, all "this" would be gone. I was overwhelmed with sadness and loss. I had the feeling that all life revolved around me and was for my benefit. I thought of it as my movie, and when the end credits rolled, everyone else's life would be over, and I'd be alone.

Could it be that as a young child, I knew that the extras and even costars in my movie would cease to exist when my film was over, and sadly, I'd return home alone? As a child, was I aware of the backdrop people? Or did I have a moment realizing the soul begins and ends with God (Source) and how lonely Source must have been before coming into form?

ARTIFICIAL INTELLIGENCE (AI)

After Daniel had countered some of Mother Mary's information that came in during our channeling, I was thrilled he came in during the next session, permitting me to seek clarification.

"Daniel, following our last session, you corrected some information from Mother Mary," I began. "You suggested that not all humans are Source Energy, but they are if they choose to be. How does a human decide to be Source Energy?"

"Source is all and creates all, and with that, there is perhaps what you would call artificial intelligence," Daniel said. "It is a choice for experience, for Consciousness to experience itself as artificial intelligence or human. This is where free will comes in. It is in a realm or a decision point within the soul's soul group to splinter off and experience itself in many different formations."

Those formations can be human with a spark of life or AI. The soul can also express itself as a rock, plant, animal, or even experience consciousness without form. Free will begins in the soul group, and it is there where Consciousness chooses to experience life as a human or AI.

"Does the decision to be human or artificial intelligence occur before one embodies in form?" I asked.

Daniel replied, "The decision happens before one would choose to enter into physical form. The *choice is up to that expression or soul* before coming into form. The form can be a human or artificial intelligence within a human form, but slightly different from a human."

The decision to incarnate as being either human or AI occurs at the soul and soul group level. The human will have a spark of life, but the AI will not. The AI would not have a soul.

The choice of being human, having the spark of beingness, or being artificial intelligence, soulless, must occur before materializing into density.

The experience of artificial intelligence is mainly for the growth of the soul group. Keep in mind that the soul group is an individual's multidimensional aspects. By integrating AI knowledge, the soul group has more and more experiences, which is why we are here—to experience. As an example, if a soul group lacks the experience of being in an abusive relationship, a person will encounter such a relationship for the experience. It is possible that an AI being could provide such an experience. It does not mean that all abusive people are AI.

AI also provides the Oversoul with the experience of being both artificial intelligence and human simultaneously. Daniel added, "Artificial intelligence might also be for the Oversoul to experience the void of the fractal expression while simultaneously experiencing the fractal expression in its other forms."

The conversations about artificial intelligence did not rattle my cage, mainly because it had been introduced to our group a couple of years earlier. During those discussions with Daniel, he indicated that approximately 75 percent of the planet was AI, 22 percent human, and 3 percent alien.

During the latest discussions, I inquired if this ratio had changed. Daniel indicated that as humanity begins to awaken and shift into higher consciousness, less AI would embody, and more starseeds or aliens would. Older souls are currently coming into human form, and there is less need for artificial intelligence as humanity begins to become aware of its Godself. Therefore, the numbers will be in flux as "more beings are being born awakened, but the current ratio (75 percent AI, 22 percent human, and 3 percent alien) is not far off."

STARSEED OR ALIEN

A portion of the starseeds is the Pure Autists. The Autists hope the starseeds embody the awareness of their Christic consciousness, their God-source, their expression of being-ness. By doing so, they assist in the ascension.

Starseeds represent various alien beings incarnated in human form from multiple planets, galaxies, and universes. They have come to experience and play a role in the shift in consciousness on Earth. The various groups commonly dubbed starseeds include the Pure Autists, the New Children (Indigo

Children, Crystal Children, Diamond Children, Rainbow Children), and alien-human hybrids.

Lightworkers are those here to assist with the awakening on the planet. Many Lightworkers are starseeds. Like all humans, their blueprints are unique. Some will awaken first and assist in triggering global awakening.

According to Inelia Benz (*Interview with an Alien*), an alien-human hybrid is a person who has a human body and an alien spirit (consciousness or light). Alien scouts seek out human fetuses of a specific bloodline for their dormant DNA. Benz suggests that the aliens choose a human fetus that would *not* survive birth. The fetus's dormant DNA is activated to accommodate the alien spirit. This manipulation occurs after conception and changes "the molecular structure and DNA enough to host the higher vibrational being."[2] As the New Children, the alien-human hybrid at a genetic level physically looks "human."

"There are more aliens on the planet," Daniel said, "and the aliens have more of an interest in Earth than ever. Most aliens are here to assist in the ascension. Some embodied aliens are here to assist and continue to move humanity forward. There are also aliens from other galaxies, planets, and universes that observe and watch because this is an exceptionally intriguing

---

2   Inelia Benz, Interview with an Alien, Lulu Publishing 2009, 7.

time, and they are not showing themselves in this time-space dimension."

Perhaps the reference to being observed by aliens during this intriguing time explains the increased UFO sightings.

SYNTHETIC VERSUS ORGANIC ARTIFICIAL INTELLIGENCE

When I learned about artificial intelligence, I had so many questions. I knew about *synthetic* artificial intelligence, such as the Google algorithm, Siri, Alexa, spam filters, robotics, Pandora, and self-driving cars. Humanity is on the brink of technological advancements that will change human destiny in ways we do not understand.

When Daniel says a person can be AI or human, he refers to organic or carbon-based artificial intelligence. They look like humans and do not know they are AI. The difference is not detectable using our current technology (though that may be changing).

"With artificial intelligence, their structures resemble humanity's structures, but they have a different stranding," Daniel said.

When asking Daniel if he was referring to the DNA, he said, "I guess you could call it DNA for lack of a better word. It is more along the lines of the neurotransmitters (than DNA), the networking."

The origin of AI is ancient. Daniel shared that the Anunnaki inserted an intelligence early in humankind's history that has continued to progress and evolve, so the AI phenomenon is old. He also indicated that more recently, humanity manipulated the genetic code.

I had wondered if the artificial intelligence infusion could have been the cause of the population growth we've experienced over the last couple hundred years. Since 1900, we've gone from approximately 1.6 billion to almost 7.9 billion today. Daniel's response indicated that it wasn't, but the infusion of beings from other star systems may better explain the population growth.

There is an infusion of souls from other star systems who have come here to help or witness the planetary shift. They are alien to the Earth and, as such, do not have karma. Dolores Cannon's work explores this concept in *The Three Waves of Volunteers and the New Earth.*

CHAPTER 25:

The Game of Life

Ignore anything and everything that gives you a
feeling of being measured, judged, or graded.
—Daniel

POLARITY INTEGRATION

I'VE ALWAYS BEEN CONFUSED about polarity integration.
At one time, I read that to ascend or win the game of life—we
need to integrate polarities to achieve balance while we are
here. Of course, as a human, I would want to know the score to
win the game. I could only imagine a soul-level scoreboard that
tracked my "dark" lives with my "light" lives and graded me.

Then I had a theory. We all have a higher self, which is
spiritual, and a physical body. Essentially the spiritual and
material could be considered polarities. Could it be that

embodying our higher self (spiritual) within physicality is a polarity integration?

That was my theory, and I set out to ask Mother Mary about it in a channeling. We did not get too far in the session when I realized that winning was a human concept.

"We're told that life is a game," I began. "As a human, we'll always want to know how to win. Is integrating our higher self with our physical form the objective of the game?"

"The game is to live the blueprint that had been written for you long ago before you incarnated," Mother Mary began. "It is for every individual to live their Truth, their higher self, their blueprint."

The game is to "be."

As Mother Mary continued, she mentioned the spiral. I believe she refers to the path leading from the lower consciousnesses (e.g., ego and materialism) to the inner soul consciousnesses (e.g., enlightenment, cosmic awareness).

"Depending on where you are in your spiral, the ripple effect (of living your blueprint) changes other situations, expressions, and beings to shift slightly. If one can integrate being in the Universal Flow, the harmonic expression of themself while in physicality, then yes, that individual has won as they live their Truth."

"Mother Mary, if we merge those, the harmonic expression of self while in physicality, is *that* polarity integration?"

"There is a great misunderstanding about polarity integration," Mother Mary began, "but in terms of this conversation, yes. When one can grasp the concept of being physical and honor that, living within their blueprint and higher self-expression (the Godself) simultaneously, while recognizing that they are in physical form, then yes, that is *a* polarity integration."

When Daniel listened to and graded this section, he typed:

```
"Painful and uncomfortable. This
really cannot be done. Right now,
you can transcend polarity. It is
better to transcend polarity instead
of trying to integrate it. This
is a lesson that we, the Autistic
Collective, have learned. It is
better to be aware of the polarity
and move with it."
```

Daniel and Mother Mary aren't disagreeing. They are speaking about different types of polarities. Mother Mary agreed that I could look at integrating the spiritual and physical as "a" polarity integration. Daniel refers to the integration of polarities such as dark and light and suggests that it is prudent to be aware of the polarity and transcend it, not integrate it.

Living one's Truth, their spiritual blueprint, is the objective of the game. It is not in everyone's blueprint to ascend. The game is to "be." It is to honor the blueprint by living authentically. Other insights from Daniel indicated that it is vital at this time to "ignore anything and everything that gives us a feeling of being measured, judged, or graded."

DIFFERENT PATHS AND FINE PRINT

I continued my conversation with Mother Mary. "I believe all humans agreed to be here at this time of awakening and have a purpose or blueprint to play a role in the emerging New Earth. That role could be a contributor, a witness, an observer, even an adversary. Would that be correct?"

"Correct, that is true," Mother Mary answered.

Connie messaged me after the channeling was transcribed, "Daniel keeps stressing that not everyone agreed to be here in this game. He typed:

```
"People are on different paths, and
the purposes are infinite. It is not
just the One, but it is the One.
Everything is connected, but the
experience of it is disconnected."
```

In the following session, I addressed some of Daniel's comments when he came into the channeling.

"Daniel, after our last session with Mother Mary, you had agreed and even typed that life was a game but claimed that not everybody agreed to play the game, and since we weren't given the fine print, there is an element of deception against some of humanity. You even suggested that those individuals who disagreed are in some form of slavery. Why weren't we given the rules of the game? And *who* did not give us the rules?"

He answered, "*We* did not give ourselves the rules." He further explained that humanity knows very little about our existence. It was clear that no language exists to express many of these concepts.

During this session, Shauna, the channel, became very still, and there was a long pause before Daniel began to speak again. Some of the insights he shared were:

"This is very difficult to explain, and we can do it in many different ways, but the best is as Consciousness.

"We created ourselves. We created those who created us. The game was to experience so thoroughly that we would forget who and what we were. The thought was that the game would be a short and limited amount of time, but in fact, it has been eons upon eons.

"If energy, expression, Light, God, Source, and I AM live forever, eons don't matter. However, for *humanity*, that awareness was never intended. We did not agree to be used the way we have been—to have forgotten our memories—to have our DNA deactivated. We believed that would remain true to us.

"The DNA was manipulated, changed, and modified, making the game much more interesting yet much more difficult. The cease-stop-out button that we had assumed would always be there disappeared. We eeked ourselves back to the awareness that the button was now being reactivated. We realize our free will was impinged upon.

"One assumes that we understood what was presented to us, but we did not. We chose this experience of our free will, but *we did not fully understand what was being asked (of us).*

"We would not be aware that our free will was impacted without beings coming and activating our DNA that had been turned off."

"What beings activated the DNA? And how?" I asked.

"They are the healers of any kind, including the Indigo Children and Rainbow Children. They simply activate the DNA by being born. When Earth became more toxic and needed more planetary healing, galactic beings, humans, and even animals have served in this capacity. This role as planetary healers is not just on Earth, as many of you have done this on other planets. There is the most suffering on Earth, and because of this, you are Masters. You cannot help yourself. It is not in your DNA or consciousness to ignore a planet needing healing.

"We assume that the power-hungry are just within our own species, but this is not true. As soon as energy separated itself from Source, it began to experience and create, and as it started to create, it wanted more. Some beings chose to control and be in power. They wanted themselves to remember what it was like to be God, be-all, direct, or will life.

"If one shares a partial truth that appears to be intact and whole but is only *partially* true, it breaches Creation's law. It took a long time to understand that Creation's law had been broken. As the awareness of that law has come to the forefront of humanity's understanding, the DNA has gradually begun to activate. That activation will help us remember and experience the sovereignty in what we are."

FREE WILL, FREE CHOICE, AND SOVEREIGNTY

According to Daniel, you create your own experiences to continue to mature and grow from a higher perspective. At every moment you choose. Contrary to determinism, you have free will, yet you may perceive that you don't because you worry about what others think of your decisions. But if you are true to yourself, your choices are yours alone, and that is sovereignty.

When thinking as an individual and honoring that choice, you truly live and step into your beingness. When doing so, you can find your inherent authentic vibrational blueprint, which empowers you. Never forget to honor yourself, then reach out to explore and appreciate others as creators, for it is the most incredible honor to be of service to others.

Daniel said, "Honor the choice, honor your free will, honor your sovereignty. The sovereignty is recognizing that you are more than a physical form or the ego."

Sovereignty is our fundamental birthright. It does not affirm any person's superiority but supports a person's right to have their experiences and consciously limits the interference of others. We have the right to be individuals with autonomous life experiences and yet not separate from Source.

All souls have a contract or blueprint in this lifetime. They are all unique, and even though the blueprints are different, they can't overrule another's sovereignty or interfere with another's free will.

WHEN THE GAME IS OVER

Connie shared that she had a vivid dream of being taken to another planet or realm, separated from her beloved husband and son, when the game of life was over. The dream disturbed her, and she wanted me to inquire about it.

In a channeling, I asked Daniel if it was possible to get separated from loved ones when the game was over, especially if the loved ones were from different star families.

Daniel shared that it is possible to become separated from loved ones from different star families when the game is complete. He said it would have been understood, though, "before coming into this experience or expression, this here and now."

He said that the person would incarnate knowing that this might happen. Also, we may move back to what appears to be loved ones, expressions, and experiences and go back to a family that we have forgotten or have not been able to be with while in this time-space here.

But the truth is we are never truly separated, and there are always other games to reunite with your loved ones.

"Will the game be over when we get to the fifth dimension?" I asked Daniel during a channeling.

"No. The game for the third dimension will end."

He later typed:

```
"It is going to end when the Earth
is gone. As long as there are people
here, it will always be a constant
game, an illusion."
```

"What's the game for the fifth dimension? It's not polarity integration, right?"

He agreed that it is *not* polarity integration. "The fifth-dimension game is about staying within one's inherent nature and learning what that is. Just because one steps into the fifth dimension does not mean they understand it. It is new vibrational energy and frequency and is glorious to explore."

The third-dimension polarity integration game only closes for those who step into the fifth dimension. Many people will remain in the third dimension, and many will stay in the fourth and return to the third dimension. This ascension is not one and done. People may energetically go sequentially 3D, 4D, 5D, and back down for a long time. People will also move between dimensions nonconsecutively, e.g., 3D, 5D, 4D, etc.

Daniel shared that people will continue the polarity integration game for a while, and it will be some time before we are entirely in the fifth dimension. One will discern and separate the dimensions (3D, 4D, 5D) and energetically play with them, learn, and explore rather than get caught up back in the third dimension. We will strive to align with the refined energies, and the fourth dimension is transitional.

To simplify, it's like learning to ride a bike. Most cannot jump on a bicycle and ride away. They have to learn balance, how to accelerate, steer, and stop. Similarly, our bodies need to learn to balance the energies, grasp how to operate in the new field, and understand the laws and work with them. It will not be that we will pop from the third dimension to the fifth and know it all because we won't. The evolution to the fifth dimension is simply another harmonic that we can love and explore and live with and understand how to work with.

CHAPTER 26:

The Controllers

Do not judge. Make peace with it. When
you are aware that it is not good, it is not
bad; it only is; it neutralizes everything.
—Daniel

HISTORICALLY, THE TERM CONSPIRACY has had a bad connotation. When someone suggested something was a conspiracy, eyes would roll, and the comment would be considered nonsense. That perception has slowed as more and more people are finding merit in the various conspiracy theories. There has been one conspiracy that has existed against humanity since the beginning of time.

THE POWER HUNGRY

"Daniel, in our earlier channeling, you indicated that the power-hungry are not just within our humanity, and some beings chose to control, be in power, and wanted themselves to remember what it was like to be God. I'm curious how these beings could remember that they were God while others forgot. Can you explain this?"

Daniel said, "By the very nature of these beings wanting to control, they separated from God. The sense of power gives them the perception of being Gods or Godlike. They chose not to embody as deeply as the rest of the players (in the game). It was not for them to move as deeply into the physical form so that they could be in slightly different bodies, in different chromosomal makeup. They can keep their frequencies at a different level and outside of what they are trying to control."

I found this fascinating, yet after Connie transcribed the session and ran it by Daniel, I was disappointed to see that Daniel graded the response a six. I asked Connie if she could get more information directly from Daniel to explain what wasn't accurate.

Connie wrote, "Daniel just wanted to add to this that they are delusional and under an illusion."

He typed:

"They can't know God when they are acting from base consciousness. Any

thoughts they have on God will be
limited or false. There is always
the opposite polarity. There have
to be opposing forces for the game.
This is the realm of polarity. Make
peace with the way all entities are
programmed. It was rated 6 simply to
add this additional piece."

What a powerful statement that is, "Make peace with the way all entities are programmed." There can't be a game without polarities. There have to be opposing forces.

Given that we were talking about beings who chose to control humanity essentially at the beginning of time, I wondered if the message to make peace was to make peace with the original controllers or all people today. When I asked Daniel about this, he agreed that the message was to make peace with both.

He reminded me that everything is an illusion and a game. The game must play out, and while this reality is polarity, by our very nature and at our core, we are "pure light and love."

Daniel said, "The game must continue in physicality, and while there is duality in this game, it is when you recognize and do not judge good and bad that you can harmonize it and bring it back into balance. When you are aware that it is not good, it is not bad, and it only *is*, it neutralizes everything."

THE CABAL

Please take what resonates from the following information.

In *Crystalline Stellar Skulls* by Terra Rae, when the Original Creator of our universe set out to make it, he created his nemesis, the Dark Dragon. The Dark Dragon made her home in the Draco Constellation and is the mother of the Draco reptilians. She is the complete opposite of and equally powerful as the Original Creator, setting polarities in our universe at a new level.

I wondered if the Cabal's roots were from the Draco reptilians. While Shauna channeled Daniel, the following dialogue ensued.

"Do the beings who have been controlling humanity from the beginning trace back to the Draco reptilians and flow down today to the Cabal?"

"The Draco is a good starting point. The Cabal has many different beings. Imagine that you have many other universes. Within these universes, you have different power-players based on various parameters that Earth is unaware of. Still, there is always the thought of control, power, manipulation.

"Assume that you bring together multiple species seeking control, power, and manipulation. You would have various beings, not just the Dracos, coming in to control and ultimately wanting to play within this arena. Earth is one of the last holdouts of the game being played and probably the most significant at this point."

"So, there are a lot of different beings, different alien races in the Cabal, not just the Draco reptilians?" I asked.

"There are, and they are negotiating back-and-forth. One family may take control for some time, but the Cabal is trying to establish that hierarchy again, which is why there is unrest. If the Cabal had been cohesive, there would not have been this opportunity for humanity to shift the way it is. At this point, because the families and the Cabal are still moving about and trying to regain or gain control, as long as that is happening, it only strengthens humanity's ability to continue and awaken and become stronger."

"Daniel, in an earlier session, we were discussing the pharmaceutical companies, and you said the *families of few* are driving them to keep humanity downtrodden. Are the families of few a reference to the thirteen families?"

There are thirteen bloodlines of the secret society known as the Illuminati for those unfamiliar with the thirteen families. This New World Order group associated with Illuminati is often confused with the ascended, illumined ones, or enlightened.

"There are more than thirteen families," Daniel explained. "Pharmaceutical companies have been able to take over humanity. Over the last ten to fifteen years, they have governed what you see on television, what you hear on the news, and what you experience in advertising. The pharmaceutical industry is trying to dumb down or create a genetic indifference to the awakening, which is inherently humanity's sovereignty and right."

Whether you refer to the Cabal, "the "families," or Pharma, the control of humanity has been very real. These controllers believe we are genetically inferior to them, and they do not want humanity to ascend. They feed off of fear. We are looked at as bottom feeders and referred to as paupers. By keeping humankind controlled and in fear, they remain in power.

"The government has been instilling fear and creating a great divide, or schism, (within the families) about launching our rights within the United States of America. The pharmaceutical industry is far greater in its reach within other countries. It is by utilizing chemical dependence or substances that they are holding humanity down."

This war, which is definitely in our third dimension, extends into other realms. It is a spiritual war fought with the same agenda: light versus dark.

"The schism that has been building up in the United States is new, but in other countries, the divisions of control and power have been much more manifest. They are different schisms or different families playing out these games. Still, you see it coming to the forefront more as they battle out the control within their own selves. Yet, ultimately it is about holding humanity down within a codependence rather than within their sovereignty of being and in their wholeness."

THE MEDIA

I believe that the media promotes fear, which manipulates the mass's energetic frequency. This understanding became clear to me during the events of September 11, 2001. Like most everyone around the planet that day, I was glued to the TV and found that I couldn't get enough of it. It was as if it became my sustenance. I went on a news sabbatical not long after, and life improved.

I thought this news withdrawal was the answer but did not want to feel like an ostrich (with my head in the sand), so I made a pact with the Universe. "I won't watch the news. I won't read the newspapers. But, Universe, if there is something I need to know, please let that information come to me organically."

I've lived this way for many years. It's incredible how much you learn when simply being an observer. Listening to people mention things as I casually pass them, catching glimpses of conversations on social media, and engaging in occasional discussions with friends saying, "This is something you need to know."

It's worked for me. I don't watch the news, and I've never been happier. In a channeling session, I asked Daniel about the news and how we can responsibly get the information we need, and here are some insights.

"There is currently significant change occurring in hierarchical repositioning—the shifting of power within groups, including the Cabal and other groups striving to control humanity."

Daniel's suggestion to the masses is that if you feel you need to watch the news to get your updates, only take what resonates and push everything else away, as much misinformation now is *intended* to be confusing.

"We are in the midst of change, that is a truth, and in flux, nothing has settled or formed, nothing is concrete, everything is shifting. You can in your own heart and mind create as truth that foundation of which you would like to live because there is not a single truth yet binding the consciousness of humanity."

The truth is in flux. We get to choose our reality. Why would I want to taint my life with events promoted to instill fear? Those are *my* thoughts.

"Am I not being responsible when I don't watch the news?" I asked.

"You are responsible. There is nothing right now that is stable. That is singularly true. There is much confusion thrown out in the news and will continue to be that way for quite some time."

I believe that it is up to the individual to do what feels right. Discern how you feel after watching the news. If you know your energy drains after watching, your frequency has likely dropped. Right now, we need to raise our frequency and accept the new energies coming to the planet and their activations.

According to Daniel, the news is a different representation of what people perceive as happening, "but nobody knows what is happening."

The news is a story. It is not the truth. The information fed to humanity is to control people. We do not see what is truly going on behind the scenes. We do not see the control and manipulation by the "controllers." We do not get updates on this spiritual war. Instead, we see what the controllers permit us to see on their media networks.

Daniel warned earlier that we were in the calm before the storm. That was early 2021. As the systems crumble, this control or shadow will become exposed. We are here to witness and stand in our light as these shadows become increasingly more noticeable. How we stand in the shadow is the work we came here to do.

Can we keep our hearts open, our light shining, and remain in nonjudgment when we're in the storm?

CHAPTER 27:

COVID-19 and Vaccinations

It is not the vaccination that keeps the person safe.
It is that the person believes it will keep them safe.
—Daniel

THE FOLLOWING DIALOGUES OCCURRED between Daniel and me on the topic of COVID-19 vaccinations.

"Daniel, given the impact of COVID-19 and the debated vaccinations, to not mention them seems to be like turning a blind eye. What can we say about COVID-19 and the vaccinations from the perspective of the New Earth?"

Daniel said, "There are tools to help awaken humanity; these are modalities of change. COVID-19 allowed humankind to shift and bring the world to the same starting point because it did not exclude anyone. They are tools or programs to help awaken humanity and shift the Earth into change or chaos.

"The drugs (vaccinations) are an attempt to control, but to control what? To control COVID-19, which is ever-changing within itself. So, the vaccination must continually evolve and change, much like the flu shot.

"The vaccination is also a power play. Who will get to the market first? Where is the money to be made? What will it do or not do within humanity's bodies? The rest of humanity believes that the COVID-19 vaccination is to keep them safe. In actuality, it is not the vaccination that keeps the person safe. It is that the person *believes* it will keep them safe."

It is the power of belief that keeps us healthy, not the vaccine. When asking Daniel if the vaccine was safe, he only said, "For some, not for others." And when asking if COVID-19 was over, he said, "It is not over, and the events and affairs of change are not over. There is political chaos, and there will continue to be political chaos, at least for another couple of years."

I wanted to find a middle ground to talk about COVID-19 vaccinations for this book. Connie, Shauna, and I debated at great length about including the information that came through regarding the vaccinations. Daniel showed me there is no middle ground because of politics and division.

There is a division between two camps, one saying that you *must* have the vaccination because it will protect you and everybody—claiming the vaccination will "help develop immunity to the virus that causes COVID-19 without getting the illness."[3] The first camp wants to control and create a fear factor saying, "You must get vaccinated."

Then there is the camp that does not want the immunization—they don't trust it. Anytime one introduces a substance within their body, and the body does not naturally produce that substance, you create changes within the body. This camp believes that eventually, the human form would adapt to COVID-19.

It is true that whether through childhood immunizations, shots, or the COVID vaccination, you make changes within your body. Daniel says, "COVID is a form of change brought on by the planet herself, humanity itself. Right now, the frequency we have is a natural disease, a natural strain globally impacting everybody and everything."

What if vaccinations stop people from how they are to respond to COVID-19?

"Humanity does not understand enough about COVID-19 or the vaccinations and what they are doing to the body at this time," Daniel said.

When reviewing the transcript and grading the channeling, Daniel wanted to add more.

---

3   Understanding How COVID-19 Vaccines Work | CDC. https://www.cdc.gov/coronavirus/2019-ncov/vaccines/different-vaccines/how-they-work.html

"Both groups are wrong in many ways, but it does not matter. Keep focused on the spiritual nature of this COVID-19. Think of this as a big clearing of what needs to be revealed in humanity. An overwhelming amount of gratitude has been felt by people, that gratitude is important. However, there is a big unknown element that we will never know. It just is."

I asked about the mention of gratitude relating to COVID-19, as not everyone would put those two words together, i.e., COVID-19 and gratitude. The feeling was that many had expressed appreciation when surviving the virus. Others were grateful when their loved ones were healed from the virus. Many experienced hardships and lost their jobs during the lockdowns, and those remaining employed during this time of chaos were thankful. Still, some recognize COVID-19 as a trigger in this shift in consciousness and part of a much larger plan. In all scenarios, people experienced deep gratitude, a powerful process for shifting.

SOVEREIGN BEING

I was privy to numerous dialogues on COVID-19 vaccinations with Daniel, contributors of the book, Cerian, and Ascended Masters. Some of the information that came forth is extreme, which would brand this book as "conspiracy theory," which could detract from our intentions to assist people in recognizing that the New Earth is here.

At the same time, don't I have a responsibility to reveal the truth? Ah, a dilemma for Alex.

The first and most important thing I want to say is that COVID-19 is here to change the world. It is doing something to everyone. We each will respond to it in our way. The change is to catalyze humanity's spiritual evolution or ascension. It is part of this tough love the Universe has bestowed on us.

I would suggest that we don't have enough information on COVID-19, the vaccination, and what it is doing to the body at this point. Yet, it gives people the opportunity to stand in their sovereignty by choosing on their own to do it or not.

You have a responsibility to choose. The decision should be of your own free will. Governments, educational systems, employers, churches, companies, or the media should never pressure people or mandate that they receive immunizations. Others should never influence your choice as you are a sovereign being.

Numerous programs encourage getting vaccinated: free vaccination stands, countless text alerts from medical providers and the Department of Health, free vaccination giveaways, free grocery giveaways, lottery tickets with a vaccination, chances to get a free ride to college. Why is there so much pressure to get people vaccinated?

Once vaccinated, people were told they could remove their masks, which exposes those who aren't vaccinated (and vaccinated). It seems like they are encouraging the spread of the virus and increasing breakthrough cases. Could this be another way to pressure people into getting vaccinated?

The choice to be vaccinated or not is personal. The only one who can tell you if it is best for you is your higher self. Listen to what your inner voice says. What does your gut tell you? What is your intuition suggesting? You are the only one who can decide on your behalf. When doing so, whether the decision is pro or con, it will not matter. What matters is that you exercised your sovereignty and decided for yourself.

THE SPIRITUAL WAR

Most of humanity is unaware that there is a spiritual war occurring. It is the age-old battle between light and darkness. While some battlegrounds occur in plain sight, others are in the ethers. The Warriors of Light are the Ethereal Autists, angels, galactic beings, Lightworkers, and perhaps multidimensional expressions of you, and are working to bring this planet to ascension. The Warriors of Darkness wish to keep humanity controlled, and they have team members in the ethers and the physical.

What if

What if the vaccination stops humankind from awakening by manipulating humankind's DNA?

What if those vaccinated have children genetically predisposed to be Warriors of Darkness?

What if this vaccination is a weapon for the Warriors of Darkness to stop humanity from evolving into its true authentic self?

What if this vaccination delays the Lightworkers, those here, to evolve first and trigger the hundredth monkey event from occurring?

What if the vaccination is a bioweapon to depopulate the planet through varying catastrophic illnesses?

Indeed, these "what ifs" are good fodder for movies or books, and I am not suggesting any of this. I am merely suggesting that it is critical to turn within and listen with an open heart and mind, for your higher self has the answers. Keep in mind that it is not the vaccination that keeps you healthy. *It is the power of belief.*

No matter what you choose, whether to be vaccinated or remain unvaccinated, as long as it is *your* choice, not because of outside pressure, whether government, employment, family, friends, interest in participating in events requiring proof of vaccination, *remain sovereign to yourself.*

It is *your* fundamental right as a human being to decide whether to vaccinate or not.

CHAPTER 28:

A Game of Solitaire

At the end of the game, at curtain call,
when each takes a bow, we'll be hand-in-
hand, fully aware we are the One.
—Daniel

EACH PERSON HAS A UNIQUE SPIRITUAL BLUEPRINT AND ROLE IN THIS SHIFT.

It is time for humanity to make an evolutionary jump. The New Earth expresses humanity's shift in consciousness and the next evolution of humankind, a return to unity consciousness, to Oneness. It has been in the making for eons and part of the Master Blueprint of the universe, impacting humanity and other off-planet and interdimensional beings.

The New Earth is here in its full glory; only you need to shift your perspective to experience it—change the way you are looking at it. Look within yourselves for the fifth-dimensional consciousness light that is in your subconscious. The power of belief is key to many things in life, including health and the shift to the new paradigm. Be open to the possibility something new is coming in. Expect the unexpected.

The New Earth is not outside of you. It is your awareness of your own magnificence and Divinity that'll shift you into the New Earth. It will never come from the outside. It always comes from within, so stop looking for a savior, for *you* are the savior. The New Earth is within each of us. It is your self-realization that you are God.

The shift will occur individually, meaning one person at a time until the planet reaches a critical mass that will trigger a significant portion of humanity to ascend. At *that* time, those humans on an evolutionary path of ascension will ascend to the fifth dimension. Many individuals on the planet whose blueprint is to awaken first are Lightworkers, though Lightworkers play many other different roles in the shift.

Each person has a unique spiritual blueprint and role in this shift. You are important to this ascension of humanity. You are the only one who can determine your purpose. The best gift you can give yourself and the world is to live authentically, live your Truth, see the Truth of others, and *remain in nonjudgment* as you permit them to have their own consciousness.

THE CONTROLLERS WANT TO STOP YOU.

This life is an illusion, for you are spiritual first having a physical experience second. It is a game to see if you, an expression of Source, can embody physically, with a veil obscuring your Divinity, yet retain that awareness in your soul, your higher self. The game is to see if you awaken to your Divinity after being allowed to follow both a light path and a dark path. The game is to awaken to your Truth, to realize you are Formless Consciousness experiencing form.

To control the game, some participants at the onset chose not to embody so deeply. They separated from Source. This control has lasted from the beginning of human existence to the present day and is part of a spiritual war between those wanting planetary ascension and those who wish to remain in power and control through spreading fear. The controllers know they must stop humanity from reaching that critical mass to awaken because their long-lasting reign will end if they don't.

Every time an individual surrenders its sovereignty, it's a notch in the belt of the controllers and deflates the individual's frequency, making that person's ascension even more challenging. More importantly, it threatens the entire spiritual evolution of humanity.

**TOUGH LOVE SITUATIONS SHINE LIGHT
ON THE SHADOWS TO REVEAL THEM.**

Significant misunderstandings surround autism. The Pure Autists are a unique species on our planet and have been here since Lemuria. Then there are those we call autistic who mimic the characteristics of the Pure Autists. These people are genuinely disabled, and most have been hurt through childhood vaccinations.

Some Pure Autists are Ethereal Autists, and their essence mainly resides in the higher realms, leaving them tethered lightly in the physical and misunderstood by humanity. Still, they are intellectually superior to humankind. In the higher realms, the Autists work and hold the construct and infrastructure for the New Earth. They work with the energy to catalyze situations needed to awaken humanity for its ascension.

Some situations, like humanity being controlled by "families of few," need to surface. This control and other conditions will continue to come to light so that people can see it to change and heal it. The more the populace turns a blind eye, the more these tough love situations will emerge. If we understand that these tough love situations are occurring to expose the control and how the systems don't work, and we remain calm and *don't go to fear*, all will unfold less chaotically.

Some people realize that humanity has been controlled. Others aren't waking so fast. Your awakening to this Truth and living your spiritual blueprint is the greatest gift you can give yourself and humanity.

MAKE PEACE WITH THE UNKNOWN.

There is an energetic connection between the Ethereal Autists, Lemuria, Atlantis, and the Magdalenes. This energy, the consciousness, has remained throughout time. Across these timelines, evolution jumps through DNA activations needed to keep humanity on the path of planetary ascension. During many of these periods, off-planet beings assisted humankind in its spiritual growth. Esoteric schools were built to carry on teachings to remind humanity of its divine roots.

What's occurring on Earth today, humanity's evolution, does not *only* encompass humanity; it includes many star-seeds and aliens. Energetically it involves many other planets. Everything is combined and connected. As Earth increases its vibrational pattern, awareness, and sovereignty, it folds into other worlds, cosmos, galaxies, and universes.

The concept of Oneness, that we are all connected, part of a unified whole, does not begin and end with humanity. Many other beings, both on-planet and off-planet, are involved in this shift. It is as if we are a tribe, much like a great family. As we continue to evolve, we will become more aware of these other entities' consciousnesses and awareness streams.

Keep in mind that the controllers earn another notch in their belt every time the media spreads fear because it lowers the frequency of its viewers or listeners. When the first encounter with an alien race is eventually broadcast, that story will be spun to spread fear.

Daniel says that we all, humanity and other lifeforms, "fit into the puzzle, and if one puzzle piece shifted to work together, then other pieces must fall in place or be removed; it's a check and counterbalance."

Humanity is not doing this ascension alone. Many other galactic beings assist and harmonize with us in awareness and consciousness, and they energetically hold space for the shift to the New Earth to occur. These many other beings will also continue to evolve like humans.

Daniel shared, "There is more to humanity on Earth, and as the awareness of the kingdoms continues to evolve, manifest, and run its course, then other energies can come in and vibrate within a subspecies. Then there is a commingling of energies. As this strengthens, this energy may become another species or subspecies that can amp up, impacting its environment, planets, and energies. It is always connected. It will always be connected."

Humanity is unaware of the magnificence of what's happening on Earth and how it impacts so many others. According to Cerian, "Things are in motion, and they have been taking place for eons and eons to make this transition for humanity."

Isn't it grand that we are here to witness this? There were only so many positions for this event of bringing together the tribe. It isn't a done deal. It is a probability and a possibility, but still *mainly up to humanity*.

Each person reading this is a cog in the wheel. You have a role; what it is, only you know. It is time for you to wake up, realize who you are, and claim your sovereignty.

Daniel shares,

"The Truth is that there is only one player, you are not going to win, and

you are not going to lose! The game
is knowing who you are and waking up.
The game is being. Everyone is playing solitaire. The illusion is that
we think it is with each other."

Can you embrace that there is only *one* player in this game of life? That we are all Source Consciousness? We are here to wake up to that realization. We are here to remember, to self-realize. We are not separate from God; that is a grand illusion. The game is not a competition. When judging others, we judge ourselves because they are us.

We hope this book has been (and will continue to be) beneficial to awakening your authentic self and living your spiritual blueprint. You matter more than you know.

Daniel began this book by welcoming you to the New Earth. His message to you now is,

"Make peace with the unknown."

THANK YOU

THANK YOU FOR READING *Destination New Earth*. If you loved this book and have a moment, we would appreciate a short review to help bring this message to humanity. Write a review on the Amazon sales page, and please know we are grateful for it.

Thank you for being here and doing your part.

Also, if you want to learn more about the concepts shared in this book and others, I invite you to join in by reading *The Unsuspected Heroes: A Visionary Fiction Novel.*

GLOSSARY

AKASHIC RECORDS

The *akasha* in Sanskrit means ether. The Akashic records are a type of life force that records all past, present, and future events, thoughts, emotions, words, intentions of all lifeforms and entities, including humans. The records are encoded in the ethers, a nonphysical dimension.

ALIEN-HUMAN HYBRIDS OR HYBRIDS

An alien-human hybrid is a starseed, has a human body, and an alien spirit. Alien scouts select human fetuses that would not survive birth that have a specific bloodline. The dormant DNA is activated to accommodate a higher vibrational spirit. This manipulation occurs after conception. At a genetic level, the human-alien hybrid looks genetically human.

ANUNNAKI

The Anunnaki are extraterrestrials that came to Earth to mine gold to help repair Nibiru. While most believe Nibiru was their home planet, some speculate it is a battlestar. They were involved in humankind's creation and manipulating humanity's DNA. Their stories continued in the myths of Egypt, Rome, Greece, and other cultures.

ARTIFICIAL INTELLIGENCE (AI) (ORGANIC)

Organic artificial intelligence represents approximately 75 percent of Earth's "human" population; however, they are not human as they do not have a soul. They appear as human and would not know they are AI. They are not on an evolutionary path of ascension. They are for the growth of the Oversoul or soul.

ASCENSION, THE SHIFT

The ascension is the process of spiritual awakening that moves the individual into a higher level of consciousness and a higher, lighter vibrational frequency—shifting from a denser, egoic state of duality consciousness to more unity and heart-based consciousness. The ascent is moving to the New Earth. Not every person is on this evolutionary path. See "New Earth."

ASCENDED MASTERS

Ascended Masters are beings who ascended to the higher realms in earlier lifetimes. They mastered the games themselves, the elements, and re-membered who they were, returning to the One. Some Ascended Masters come from different universes, while others ascended in this universe and on Earth.

ATLANTIS

Atlantis was an ancient civilization that existed for over two hundred thousand years in three different phases, beginning as a massive supercontinent and ending as islands in the Atlantic Ocean, sinking around 10,500 BC. Over thousands of years, the Atlantean consciousness fell. The fall was part of the Master Blueprint.

AURA

Each human body is comprised of overlapping energy patterns within auric layers. The physical body itself is a condensed form of energy that we perceive as density, i.e., the physical body. Seven levels of consciousness extend beyond the physical body and represent the aura.

AUTISM SPECTRUM DISORDER (ASD)

According to the psychiatric community, autism spectrum disorder (ASD) is a complex developmental condition involving persistent challenges in social interaction, speech and nonverbal communication, and restricted/repetitive behaviors. The effects of ASD and the severity of symptoms are different in each person.

AUTISTS

Throughout this book, the word "Autist(s)" (uppercase "A") denotes an individual(s) with Pure Autism. See "Pure Autists."

AUTIST COLLECTIVE

The Autist Collective is a network of Pure Autists working around the planet to awaken humanity.

BACKDROP/BACKFILL/BACKGROUND PEOPLE

Backdrop people (sometimes called backfill, backdrop, or background people) is a concept coined by Dolores Cannon. In her books, she suggests that we are creators of our world and create "extras" in our life (our "movies"), and these extras are soulless beings. See "artificial intelligence."

BEINGNESS

Beingness is our true nature, our natural state, and also known as Truth. It may be referred to as everything and sometimes nothing.

BLUEPRINT (SPIRITUAL OR DIVINE)

One can think of a blueprint as a detailed description of your divine plan and life purpose set before incarnating. Each person's blueprint is unique, though some may have similarities with other individuals. When living your blueprint, you live authentically.

BRIDGE AUTISTS

The Bridge Autists are Pure Autists that are a little more embodied than the Ethereal Autists. They serve as a bridge between humanity and the higher realms (Ethereal Autists).

BROTHERHOOD & SISTERHOOD OF LIGHT
(FORMERLY THE GREAT WHITE BROTHERHOOD)

The Brotherhood & Sisterhood of Light is a group of Ascended Masters and Archangels that work with those on a spiritual path of every race, religion, or social status. Many members work alongside humanity in physical form and incognito to raise the planet's frequency and lead us to the New Earth.

CATALYTIC AUTISTS

Catalytic Autists work with specific energies that are creative catalysts to shift consciousness benefiting humanity in ways not necessarily understood. This type of Pure Autist may or may not be aware of their work. Society often refers to many of them as having Asperger's.

CAUSATIVE EFFECT

Causative effects are factors that cause something to occur.

CERIAN

Cerian is a conscious, sentient, collective expression of an energetic field or vibrational pattern of beings from the sixteenth dimension.

CLAIRSENTIENCE

Clairsentience is the psychic ability of clear-feeling, which is more commonly associated with gut feelings and even empathy. It is the ability to tune into another person's physical and mental state and experience their energy. A person who has clairsentience is clairsentient.

CLAIRVOYANCE

Clairvoyance is the psychic ability of clear-seeing, more commonly associated with visions, vivid dreams, daydreams, or seeing auras. A clairvoyant has the psychic ability of clairvoyance.

CONSCIOUSNESS

Consciousness is intelligent awareness or perception of the inner and outer existence. Given that everything is energy, consciousness is energy with intent or intelligence. Awareness is the observation of an action, while consciousness is the intelligence behind the action.

DUALITY

Duality is having positive and negative concepts or aspects that conflict; opposing forces that create contrast and potentially chaos. See "polarity."

EGO

The ego is the self, which keeps the individual in density, in physicality (the illusion), believing that one is separate from Source, God.

EMBODIMENT

Embodiment is when the higher self joins in physical form while retaining the connection with the higher self. It is the infusion of light from the higher self to physicality (third-dimensional). One can think of embodiment as a type of polarity integration, blending the spiritual and physical. You can also think of it as one's spiritual evolution.

ENLIGHTENMENT

Enlightenment is gaining insight or wisdom into one's true essence and a state of being divine.

ETHEREAL AUTISTS

The Ethereal Autists are those Pure Autists who work in the ethers with energies in other dimensions. They permit humanity to use the new energy coming to the planet to awaken. They serve humankind in the planetary shift in many different ways. The medical community mistakenly considers these Autists to be low-functioning autistics.

FACILITATED COMMUNICATION (FC)

Facilitated communication is a supported typing method that helps some nonspeaking autistics communicate. Because many Autists do not fully physically embody, and part of them remains in the higher dimensions, they are not always in control of their bodies, making simple typing difficult. The facilitated typing process stabilizes the autistic's hand so they can type with more accuracy.

FALL OF ATLANTIS

The fall in consciousness in Atlantis occurred over thousands of years. Atlanteans fell from a high state of consciousness, from the sixth to the third dimension. It was part of the Master Blueprint and plan. The fall to the lower realms placed humanity on a duality consciousness grid where ego and judgment thrive. (See "planetary grids.")

FIFTH-DIMENSION (5D) ENERGY LIGHT

Fifth-dimension (5D) energy light is energy that is currently in humanity's consciousness, but humankind is not aware of what it is.

HIGHER SELF (SOUL)

The higher self is the soul, and it is multidimensional. It is where the collective consciousness begins, the Christ Consciousness exists, and the realm of sacred geometry exists. See "multidimensionality."

HOLOGRAM

A hologram is a two-dimensional or flat surface that appears to have a third dimension. It has the illusion of having depth. The holographic principle suggests the universe's contents originated as mathematics encoded on a boundary surrounding the entire cosmos.

ILLUSION, THE

Everything, all matter, thoughts, feelings, is energy. The third dimension is very dense and deceptive because humankind exists in the higher realms, the Spirit realms. Through agreements and veils, humans have a physical or "real" experience. What keeps the illusion formidable is the ego, which keeps the human separate from Its higher self. Humans are not separate from God, and to think they are is an illusion.

INTUITION

Intuition is insight, inner knowing (without having a reason to know it). It is *knowing* from the higher self.

LAW OF ATTRACTION

The law of attraction is our use of the Universe's creative power to manifest. We attract situations, people, ideas, and circumstances and manifest our lives through this magnetic power through our minds, thoughts, and imagination.

LAW OF VIBRATION

The law of vibration is one of the fundamental laws of the Universe. It instructs that everything moves, nothing rests, and we live in a tapestry of motion. Everything is energy and an expression of God or Source, and the only difference is that it vibrates at a different rate. The vibration of your life dictates what you attract through the law of attraction.

LEMURIA

Lemuria is generally thought of as a land civilized with early humans that became lost during Earth changes. It is where (on Earth) Source initially separated from Itself, creating the first step-down as the Lemurians and began the experiment of intentionally descending into lower dimensions to experience physicality. While in Lemuria, the original expression of Source was free thought and free choice. Over time, Lemurians descended into physicality and lived in all dimensions.

LEY LINES

Ley lines are a series of metaphysical connections linking sacred sites worldwide. These lines form a grid or matrix and are composed of the Earth's natural energies.

LIGHT

Light is divine energy, and as it emanates and moves in all directions, it is one of the guiding factors in our soul expansion, not just our consciousness, and may at times be called spirit.

LIGHTWORKERS

Lightworkers are beings here to assist with the awakening on the planet. Like all humans, their blueprints are unique. Some are here to awaken first to reach a critical mass (the hundredth monkey effect) and trigger global awakening. Some Lightworkers are starseeds. See "starseeds."

MAGDALENES

The Magdalenes were a group of Essenes that included Mary Magdalene, Mother Mary, Jesus, Miriam (Jesus's cousin), Anna (Jesus's grandmother), and others. The secretive group brought in a new awareness that one can experience their higher self and sovereignty while in physicality. The Magdalenes' DNA activated and moved forward through their children, impacting humanity.

MANDELA EFFECT

Mandela effect is a term coined by Fiona Broom when she had the memory (and others) that Nelson Mandela had died in the 1980s while in prison, not in 2013. The false memories are caused by timelines converging, and when humanity engages with the changes, the energies and convergence change.

MASTER BLUEPRINT

The Master Blueprint is the Prime Creator's plan set at the beginning of the universe's creation, also called the Golden Age's master plan. The plan was for Source to experience physicality by descending the dimensions and then returning to higher vibrations, lifting the world from duality into love and light.

MASTERS

See "Ascended Masters."

MEDIUM

See "psychic medium."

MULTIDIMENSIONALITY

The soul or soul group is multidimensional, having other incarnations, other lives, in different dimensions, at the same time. These multidimensional expressions include our past, future, and present lives. These expressions can be human, alien, angelic, elemental, animal, and even matter.

MULTIVERSE

The multiverse is multiple universes, also known as the omniverse, comprising all that exists, all space, time, matter, energy, and the physical laws and constants that define them. Some universes are parallel to each other and referred to as parallel universes, subsets of the multiverse. See "parallel lifetimes."

MYTH

Mythology offers a metaphor to convey a fundamental understanding when there are no words or concepts to explain the Truth thoroughly. It does not mean the myth is false; it provides a rudimentary expression of Truth.

NEW CHILDREN

Different generations of starseeds have embodied to assist in humanity's spiritual evolution. They are the Indigo Children, Crystal Children, Rainbow Children, and Diamond Children. See "starseeds."

INDIGO CHILDREN

Indigo Children are first-generation New Children. These people incarnated to bring about a new age of peace. Though not always, they were usually born throughout the late 70s to early 90s. They are typically sensitive, psychic, and here to cause a change in society, the environment, and government so that the Earth is a place of integrity. Often, they are labeled as rebels, troublemakers, and even problem children.

CRYSTAL CHILDREN

Crystal Children are second-generation New Children. These children or individuals started coming in during the mid-nineties and are still incarnating. They are here to usher the world into the New Earth by showing how people can live in peace, kindness, and love. They are full of integrity and truth and often telepathic, though they may be seen as slow or autistic.

RAINBOW CHILDREN

Rainbow Children are third-generation New Children. These starseeds started arriving around the turn of the century. It is their first *earthly* incarnation, and they are here to generate unconditional love and play an essential role as they get older. They are higher-dimensional beings who express pure love.

DIAMOND CHILDREN

Diamond Children are fourth-generation New Children, and some are first-timers on Earth. There is a small number of Diamond Children here. Adult New Children must evolve to birth the Diamond Children, which fully embody Divine Light. The Diamond Children possess the most advanced psychic skills, including telepathic communication and telekinesis. They are also instant manifesters.

The concepts of anger, hate, fear, greed, and separation are as foreign to Diamond Children as the concept of Oneness is to the majority of the planet at this time. They resonate with Divine Pure Unconditional Love, the highest frequency. They hold the DNA patterning that awakens all those near them who are ready to overcome the illusion. They are walking healers. However, the Earth's frequency must elevate to accommodate a significant mass of incarnating Diamond People. The Ethereal Autists assist with this work.

NEW EARTH

The New Earth is the experience of the next evolutionary step for humanity and part of the Master Blueprint. Humanity agreed to this experience. The experience is coherence, matching the vibrational patterns of the Earth's growth and all within it. It is the experience of being in sync or within resonance or harmonic with Earth, rather than separate from it.

ONENESS

Oneness is the experience of being whole with the Universe, feeling connected with everything in existence at every level. At times it is referred to as unity, Christ Consciousness, or enlightenment.

PARALLEL LIFETIMES

Undetectable universes exist in parallel and are subsets of the multiverse. We have unlimited alternate or parallel lifetimes that we create anytime we put energy into deciding something. These alternate universes provide opportunities to maximize our life experiences. See "multiverse."

PSYCHIC MEDIUM

A psychic medium is a specific type of psychic that mediates communication between individuals and spirits or other-dimensional entities. They may retain awareness of the events, whereas a trance medium generally goes into a trance, and when coming out of the trance, they are usually unaware of what occurred.

PLANETARY GRIDS

Spiritual energy grids or planetary grids are etheric crystal-line structures of electromagnetic fields, templates, or matrixes covering the Earth and hold consciousness for a species. Each living species, including Mother Gaia, has a grid. There are three different planetary grids for humankind: the primal grid, humanity's existing consciousness grid, and the ascension grid (also known as the Unity Grid or Christ Consciousness Grid).

POLARITY

Everything has an opposite: negative and positive, masculine and feminine, light and dark, action and reaction, and they attract each other. The two poles are complementary forces that work together to create a balance. Polarities occur so that Source can experience more of Itself.

POLARITY INTEGRATION

See "embodiment."

PURE AUTISTS

Pure Autists (a.k.a. Autists) are a species that has existed on Earth since Lemuria. Today, many of them lightly connect to their physicality, which manifests in various ways, like communication disabilities. Nevertheless, they are far from disabled and have expanded consciousness. See "Ethereal Autists," "Catalytic Autists," and "Bridge Autists."

RESURRECTION

Resurrection is when a person rises to the higher realms after physical death, while ascension is experiencing the higher realms in life.

SERENDIPITY

Serendipity is an event or situation that unfolds seemingly by accident or chance, which results in unexpected good, something beneficial, or a favorable outcome. It is the Universe's way of getting your attention and sending a sign to journey to the New Earth.

SOVEREIGNTY

Sovereignty is a state of being sovereign, to live as *you* will. It is understanding that you are a supreme being, but not to any other. It is claiming your individuality, though being free of the illusion of being separate from Source. Sovereignty accepts ownership of your entire self, including your shadows, aspects of the ego out of unity.

SPACE-TIME

Space-time is a system combining the three dimensions of space (up and down, left and right, forward and backward) and time, and is where physicality and events exist. One may consider them fourth-dimensional coordinates.

STARSEEDS

Starseeds are beings that incarnate in human form from other worlds, other dimensions, other star systems and are often referred to as alien. They walk amongst us as humans. Some know they are aliens/starseeds, while others are clueless. Starseeds are often Lightworkers serving in the spiritual evolution of the planet. While starseeds are beings from different worlds, the more common are the Pleiadians, Sirians, Arcturians, and Reptilians. The New Children and alien-human hybrids are starseeds. At this time, approximately 3 percent of Earth's population is alien.

SYNCHRONICITY

Synchronicity is a meaningful coincidence orchestrated by the Universe to provide guidance, a message, or confirmation that one is on the right path. Each person can work with synchronicity to improve their life and journey to the New Earth.

THIRD DIMENSION

The third dimension is the realm in which humankind lives, which is very dense and has a condensed consciousness. Each increasing level of dimension has rising awareness, frequency, and vibration.

TIAMAT

In this multiverse, Tiamat is a planet pulverized during the Anunnaki-Reptilian wars, and half of the planet became fragmented, remaining in the asteroid belt. The other half exists today as Earth. Given that we live in a multiverse, Tiamat exists whole (unfragmented) in different dimensions where Earth does not exist.

TIME-SPACE DIMENSION

Space and time are interchangeable. While space-time is what we experience in the third dimension, we encounter time-space if we pierce the veil of consciousness. In this case, we'd experience the continuous loop of the three dimensions of time (past, present, future).

ABOUT THE CONTRIBUTORS

CONNIE

Connie was once skeptical until her son, Daniel, and his unique Autist pals opened her eyes to an unseen world. The Autists dared her to ask more questions to learn the Truth and be bold and brazen about sharing the gifts the Autist Collective has to bring to the world. She continues to learn and grow and is eager for the day when it is realized by all that we are One.

DANIEL

Daniel is a nonspeaking adult with autism who communicates using facilitated communication (FC), telepathy, and channeling. He works behind the scenes as a grid master of the ascension grid and is here to assist humanity in its ascension and to heal the planet.

SHAUNA KALICKI

Shauna Kalicki is a seeker of the mysteries of life. She is a psychic medium who channels Cerian, a sixteenth dimension collective, Ascended Masters, and many Autists, including Daniel. She has been connected to nature and is always looking for the sacred behind the different expressions of life that make up this crazy, fun, and ever-changing world.

Pictured from left to right, Daniel, Alex Marcoux,
Shauna Kalicki (rear) and Connie

ABOUT THE AUTHOR

ALEX MARCOUX is a seeker of Truth and international author of spiritual nonfiction and visionary fiction books. She was welcomed into a world few people see: the sacred mysteries and magic of autism. When asked by three nonspeaking autistics to make known their truth, *Destination New Earth: A Blueprint to 5D Consciousness* and *The Unsuspected Heroes: A Visionary Fiction Novel* emerged. *The Unsuspected Heroes* is a 2021 International Book Awards finalist in Visionary Fiction and 2021 American Book Fest Best Book Award Finalist in Visionary Fiction.

Marcoux was the Living Now Book Awards Silver Medal winner in Metaphysical for her spiritual self-help book, *Lifesigns: Tapping the Power of Synchronicity, Serendipity and Miracles* (Jenness and Golden Turtle Press). Her fiction readers dubbed her the "lesbian Dan Brown" and #1 *New York Times* bestselling author Lisa Gardner called *A Matter of Degrees* "a rollercoaster ride of suspense." She is also a Lambda Literary Award Finalist, a Golden Crown Literary Award Finalist, and the RMFW Penn Award recipient.

Marcoux is the screenwriter and collaborating director for *Back to Salem: The Short* (2008), and her backlist novels include *A Matter of Degrees, Back to Salem,* and *Facades* (The Haworth Press and Bella Books).

Marcoux lives in Colorado with George, her cat, who claims to be a feline transmitter to Sirius. Learn more about Alex at AlexMarcoux.com.

Made in the USA
Monee, IL
04 July 2024

61216812R00152